Catfishing in the South

Jeff Samsel

OUTDOOR TENNESSEE SERIES
Jim Casada, *Series Editor*

THE UNIVERSITY OF TENNESSEE PRESS / Knoxville

Catfishing in the South

GRM (~1

The Outdoor Tennessee Series covers a wide range of topics of interest to the general reader, including titles on the flora and fauna, the varied recreational activities, and the rich history of outdoor Tennessee. With a keen appreciation of the importance of protecting our state's natural resources and beauty, the University of Tennessee Press intends the series to emphasize environmental awareness and conservation.

Copyright © 2003 by The University of Tennessee Press / Knoxville. All Rights Reserved. Manufactured in the United States of America. First Edition.

All photographs by Jeff Samsel unless otherwise noted.

This book is printed on acid-free paper.

Library of Congress Cataloging-in-Publication Data

Samsel, Jeff.
Catfishing in the South/Jeff Samsel.— 1st ed.
    p. cm.—(Outdoor Tennessee series)
ISBN 1-57233-235-2 (pbk.: alk. paper)
1. Catfishing—Southern States.
 I. Title.
II. Series.
SH691.C35 S26 2003
799.1'7492—dc21   2003005695

To Sarah and Nathaniel,
my two favorite
catfishing buddies

Contents

Chapter 1. Major Species

Chapter 2. Catfish Waters

Chapter 3. Bait and Tackle

Chapter 4. Catfishing Strategies

Chapter 5. Southern Hotspots

Appendixes

Editor's Foreword

My first experience with catfish left a powerful, poignant memory. It came when I was five or six years old. My family had joined another family for a weekend of camping, fishing, and relaxation on Fontana Lake, near my boyhood home of Bryson City, North Carolina. After supper one evening my father and his friend fished from a boat just offshore while I sat astraddle an old stump just above the water line. My angling equipment was of the simplest possible sort—a well-cured cane pole equipped with black nylon line, a bobber, and a hook baited with worms.

The fishing was wonderful. Hefty, hungry bream zeroed in on my offering with satisfying regularity, and when the bobber vanished I would heave back on the pole with all my strength. The result was the satisfying sight of another bluegill arcing through the air to land on the bank behind me, where the fish would quickly be transferred from hook to stringer.

After a dozen or so fish, the bobber dipped from sight with unprecedented alacrity, and my reaction produced no movement whatsoever in the long, limber can pole. Indeed, when I heaved, the tip of the pole bent and then plunged into the water. Had my thighs not been wrapped around the stump that served as my fishing spot, something would surely have had to give. Either I would have turned loose of the pole or been unceremoniously dragged into the lake. As it was, the tug of war was roughly equal, although I yelled for help with sufficient volume that my father declares, to this day, that the sound echoed off the mountains on the opposite side of the lake.

Assistance soon arrived in the form of two bemused adults, and fortunately the rope-like braided nylon line held fast. A few minutes later the battle was won, and a glistening channel cat that probably would have gone a third of my weight lay on the shore. I don't recall exactly what happened after that, although I'm sure that the white, tasty fillets from the fish provided a hearty meal cooked atop a Coleman stove the following day.

Again relying on my father's recollections (and I now know that he must have been almost as pleased as he was when I finally, a few years later, managed to catch my first trout on a fly), I indulged in the timeless fisherman's prerogative of "bragging rights." He declares that my first words were: "Boy, catching a big one sure makes your knees shake." That seems entirely credible to me, because coming to grips with a real bruiser of a back-alley brawler in the form of a trophy catfish still means an adrenaline rush and great excitement for me.

My reaction, then and now, has become one that an increasing number of anglers share. In this book Jeff Samsel, an exceptionally promising young sporting scribe who has established himself in a solid niche as a catfishing expert, offers insight and information on why this is the case. In a marvelously misspent life in angling, one that has involved catfish adventures stretching across portions of six decades, I have dealt with Mr. Whiskers in a variety of ways. These have included running trotlines from a poled flat-bottom boat, checking limblines on a daily basis, catching the fish by hand when they were in automobile tires during the spawning period, and sportfishing. Yet upon finishing these pages the realization dawned that my catfishing education had, at best, reached the kindergarten stage. These pages are a primer that bid fair to change that educational level.

Just as they've been an integral part of my sporting life, in Tennessee, and the same holds true across the South, catfish have long figured in the human equation. In low-water conditions of late summer and early fall, especially in periods of drought such as those that have persisted over much of the region in recent years, vestiges of fish traps used by Native Americans can still be found. Indeed, to return once more to the halcyon years of my boyhood, I recall adults pointing out such traps in shoals along the Little Tennessee River. Even to my youthful mind, the obvious labor required to make these long funnels comprised of thousands of large rocks was impressive. I had somewhat similar experiences in damming creeks to make faster runs for tubing and realized that the Cherokees who fashioned the devices would not have done so unless they expected appreciable return. With women and children splashing through the water to drive fish and the men taking them from the trap as they crowded into its ever narrowing mouth, the undertaking was a community effort combining pleasure with practicality.

The dividends for the Indians' efforts took the form of a rich bounty of channel catfish, with the edible portions furnishing fine culinary fare and the rest doubtless being used as fertilizer for corn, squash, and beans in rich bottomlands. The Cherokees also used concoctions such as crushed black walnut husks and other vegetative matter to poison, stun, or otherwise disable the fish so that they could be harvested.

European pioneers also relied on catfish as an important item of diet, catching them with hook and line, by hand (grappling or noodling), in baited traps made from slender strips of cane, and in other ways. Later, other means of procurement included sticks of dynamite, electrical charges produced with various hand-cranked devices, trotlines, throwlines, limblines and jug fishing.

Obviously little if any sport was involved. This was subsistence fishing, and along major waterways such as the Mississippi and Tennessee Rivers, hardy souls known as "river rats" or "river men" earned a hardscrabble living from catching and selling catfish. Even in the little mountain community I called home, there was a local character, "Old Al," who specialized in taking catfish. He would catch them, keep them in a wire cage in a branch for a couple of weeks to "clean them out" (the Tuckaseegee River was, at the time, terribly polluted by an upstream pulp plant), feed them corn kernels and meal, and then sell the catfish. A rough and ready cat-fishing subculture once existed over much of the South.

Although times have changed dramatically, the fish still fill an important socioeconomic niche. Salt and pepper catfish and catfish fillets are featured menu items at rural fish camps, and a meal of these delicacies, on bulging plates flanked by a batch of hushpuppies and slaw, guarantees tears of pure joy in the eyes of a country-boy gourmet. Today the makings of these meals come from intensive aquaculture operations as opposed to wild waters, and another notable change has paralleled the growth of the catfish industry.

Recreational angling has brought about the transition from catfish being viewed as trash fish to their being prized, with trophy-sized fish being routinely released. Where a generation or two ago many sportsmen viewed catfish with near-total disdain, today everything from half-pound bullheads to behemoth-class flatheads and blue cats weighing up to a hundred pounds are objects of great interest. Commercial stinkbaits, all sorts of rods, reels, and rigs designed with catfish specifically in mind, and guide operations focusing on catfish abound. Catfish tournaments, while far from rivaling the glitz and glamour associated with professional bass fishing, are growing rapidly in popularity.

Jeff Samsel chronicles these developments in considerable depth, and the end result is a volume no serious devotee of Mr. Whiskers can afford to ignore. From hard-core how-to information in the form of countless tips and effective techniques to detailed coverage of where to find the finest in catfishing, he leads the reader down lazy rivers and to the base of roiling tailraces.

A number of features distinguish this book, setting it apart from general works on the subject. One is its regional focus. While the upsurge of interest in "catching cats" over the last two decades has resulted in the predictable publication of several books on the subject, heretofore none has focused specifically on Tennessee and the South. In that sense Samsel's volume is long overdue. After all, catfish have long loomed large in southern literature and song. One only has to remember the exploits of Mark Twain's Huck Finn or any number of country songs with lines recounting lazy summer days spent along creek banks waiting for a bobber to bounce.

Another important aspect of the work, and it is one that goes hand-in-hand with its inclusion in the Outdoor Tennessee series, is the author's concern with the catfish and its home waters from an environmental perspective. In that regard, we are given a solid look at the historical roots of catfishing, the habits and preferred habitat of this homely (some would say flat-out ugly) denizen of the deep, and many of the myriad concerns associated with the future of catfish and the waters where they live.

As the life blood of the good earth, creeks, rivers, and lakes offer a ready way to monitor the health of the land. Along similar lines, as bottom feeders, catfish can be the watery equivalent of the traditional coal miner's canary. These are concerns well deserving of our awareness, but arguably the single most important message found in the pages that follow transcends their environmental and recreational coverage. As we read of effective methods to catch catfish, the individuals who have mastered these methods, and the places where they can be employed, we find ourselves doing some time travel. Or at least that was the case with this reader.

I was transported back to a delightful time of simpler days and simpler ways, when catfish-filled rivers ran through my life and a nearby lake carried alluring promise of doing battle with a real lunker. The passage of many years may mean I am viewing those slow-paced summers of youth through rose-colored lenses. Even if such is the case, the underlying reality remains the same. Namely, fishing offers a wonderful way to soothe the troubled soul and escape the pressures of the hurly-burly pace of today's world. Izaak Walton, whose literary musings rank him as a sort of patron saint for the fisherman, put it well when he wrote in *The Compleat Angler*, "Doubt not but angling will prove to be so pleasant that it will prove to be, like virtue, a reward to itself."

Share the lure and lore of angling with youngsters, and you give them not one but many rewards that will last a lifetime. They will know simple pleasure, inner peace, and a closeness to and appreciation of the good earth. Those themes run as a strong undercurrent throughout this book, and the author would readily acknowledge that one of his great joys in life is sharing angling with his two children. Children such as his are the ultimate hope for protection and preservation of the natural world, and there are few better ways to introduce them to the wonders of sport than through catfishing. This book takes us to pleasant places, locales full of promise for fruitful fishing, and in doing so reminds us of the delight to be found in the simple phrase, "gone fishin'." Or, to conclude with further words from Walton:

> Oh, the gallant fisher's life!
> It is the best of any;
> 'Tis full pleasure, void of strife,
> And 'tis beloved by many.

—Jim Casada
Series Editor

Preface

Using satellite signals collected and interpreted by his electronic fish finder, an angler motors straight to a potentially productive spot. From the lake's surface, the spot appears to be in the middle of nowhere. Twenty feet beneath, however, the old river channel makes a hard bend through a deep hole, and hefty flathead catfish often stack up around the brush that litters the bottom of the hole.

Upon arriving, the angler will ride repeatedly over the spot, searching for big catfish with his graph. If he finds enough fish to give him confidence in the hole, he will set two anchors to position his boat precisely and then put down several live baits, kept fresh in a large circular bait tank. He has heavy braided line spooled on high-quality conventional reels, all matched with rods designed specifically for battling big catfish.

While barefoot boys will always sit on creek banks putting out night crawlers with cane poles and wrestling channel catfish from creek-bend pools, the overall face of catfishing went through a major transition during the latter part of the 20th century—and that transition continues today. Cats have become important sport fish on many rivers and lakes throughout the South, and they are finally being recognized for more than their frying-pan qualities, which, incidentally, are unrivaled in the minds of many anglers and non-anglers alike.

The fishing record books provide some of the best evidence of how catfishing has developed into a serious sport. The blue catfish world record was broken three times in the 1990s and again in 2000, and the flathead record was upped by more than 30 pounds in 1998 by a fish caught in Kansas. Line-class records, meanwhile, are rewritten almost monthly for all three major catfish species.

Today's catfisherman will travel far from home to a destination like Santee Cooper or the Tennessee River in search of giant flat-heads and blues, and the quality of his gear will match that of any tournament bass fisherman.

Records are certain to continue falling as anglers become bet-ter acquainted with the habits and habitats of catfish, the best waters for giant catfish throughout the South, and the techniques and tackle required to locate, hook, and land the big cats. Historical commercial catches show that flatheads and especially blues can grow much larger than what has been landed so far by rod and reel.

As rich a heritage surrounds catfish as any variety of fresh-water fish in the southeastern United States. Cats of various kinds abound in streams and lakes of every size throughout the region and have provided sustenance as long as humans have occupied what is now known as the South. Long before the first catfish was ever landed with a rod and reel, various forms of fish traps, spears, and lines were used first by American Indians and then by early settlers.

Catfishing heritage also falls into the realm of folklore, simply because of the sizes that flathead and blue catfish reach. Commer-cial catches throughout the first half of the 1900s commonly yielded catfish that tipped scales well past the 100-pound mark, and legend says that many divers doing work on big-river dams have refused to return to the depths after seeing catfish that were larger than them.

Today, catfish rank among the most popular sport fish in the nation. In 1996, of the 29 million anglers who fished in freshwater, 7.4 million fishermen spent 91 million days trying to catch catfish, according to the National Survey of Fishing, Hunting and Wildlife-Associated Recreation conducted by the U.S. Fish and Wildlife

Service. Nowhere is the sport more popular than in the South, where major rivers like the Mississippi, Missouri, and Cumberland and reservoirs like Texoma and the Santee Cooper lakes produce some of the nation's finest catfishing.

Only a handful of books have been written with catfishermen in mind, compared to dozens—maybe hundreds—of titles devoted to fishing for bass or trout. Much of what has been published over the years, mostly in magazines, has lumped the catfish species together and generalized the fishing information. Catfishermen, consequently, have tended to generalize their approaches to catching cats.

Only recently have more anglers begun to understand how different flatheads are from blues, how different working a tailwater is from fishing the lake above it, and that catfish can be caught at any time other than on a summer night.

This book is written for everyone who fishes for catfish in the South, whether brand-new to the sport or a lifelong catfish angler. The first half lays foundations, exploring the history of catfishing in the region, and drawing distinctions between catfish species, types of waterways where catfish are found, and the kinds of gear needed for various styles of catfishing. The last two chapters, covering strategies and Southern hotspots, are more specific and detailed and generally build on what earlier chapters offer.

"The South" means different things to different people. This book includes coverage from 14 different states, all of which are either distinctly Southern or commonly associated with the South and Southern culture. The most westerly state is Texas; the most northerly are Missouri and West Virginia.

This book is not exclusively about how and where to catch giant catfish, but there is an admitted big-fish bias in the approaches and the locations that are given the most attention. Big catfish provide big sport, and the enormous size potential of these fish is a major part of the appeal of fishing for them. Also, as is true with any species, big cats have been around the block a time or two. Hooking one often demands a refined approach. Landing one allows almost no room for error.

While I fish for almost everything that swims on occasion, I am an avid catfishermen, and I have fished for channels, flatheads, blues, and bullheads throughout the South. I don't claim to be an expert on the sport, but I've spent a fair number of hours in boats and on banks with folks who deserve that label.

Some hotspot and strategy chapters use specific sources to tell about the places these experts have spent their lives fishing or a unique way they often target cats. However, the entire book, in fairness, is a collection of insights from dozens of very skilled cat-fishermen, many of whose names I never even knew.

Beyond hard information on how and where to catch catfish in the South, I hope this book conveys an appreciation for catfish and the need to maintain our rivers and lakes in fit condition for fish to live in.

I even think catfish are pretty, but I don't expect to convince everyone who reads this book of that!

Acknowledgments

Thank you first to my grandpa for teaching me to fish and to my parents for nurturing interests in fishing and in writing.

Special thanks to Terry Madewell, who first introduced me to heavyweight catfish; to Keith "Catfish" Sutton, who shares my passion for cats and has helped out in many ways with this book; and to Tom Evans, who helped enormously with fulfilling photo needs.

Thank you to Jim Casada, who encouraged me to write *Catfishing in the South* and helped get the project under way, and to the University of Tennessee Press for choosing to include this book in the Outdoor Tennessee series.

Thank you also to many catfishermen—far too many to even begin naming—whose collective "research" underlie this work, and to those fisheries, biologists, agencies, and organizations who have invested in catfish research and who work hard to take care of our rivers and lakes.

Thank you to my wife Denise and children, Sarah and Nathaniel, for their unfailing support as I have worked on my "catfish book," and to many friends for their encouragement and prayers.

Most of all, I give thanks to Jesus Christ, my Lord and Savior, through whom all the catfish and the waters they swim in were created.

Introduction

Food for the Table

Folks who don't fish generally don't know much about fish. Most people wouldn't know a bass from a trout, nor the habitats preferred by either. One thing that virtually everyone knows about fish, however, is that catfish taste good.

In the South, especially, catfish rank high on the list of favorite foods. Fried catfish stands out as popular Friday night restaurant fare and serves as the main course for many a church social. The meat is firm, mild, and sweet, and well-suited for frying, baking, or grilling.

Beyond the actual eating qualities, fine as they are, some of the popularity of catfish as Southern table fare undoubtedly stems from their widespread availability. Catfish of various sorts abound in creeks, lakes, and rivers throughout the South.

Whether by rod and reel, jugs or limblines, most Southern sportsmen know of a spot or two not far from home where they can go have fun catching catfish and bring home good groceries in the process. If they live near waters inhabited by blues or flatheads, they also know that even a single fish could provide several fine meals.

The availability of catfish, along with the large sizes they grow to, their high caloric count, and the relative ease by which they can be captured has made catfish popular food fish for several centuries in the South. As Charles Hudson noted in *The Southeastern Indians*, catfish are believed to have been among the most important food fish for Indians in the Southeastern United States. The gear commonly used by Indians to catch cats included predecessors to modern trotlines and limblines, both of which used hooks made from deer or turkey bones.

Some Indians were also bow-fishermen, shooting arrows tied to lines with wooden floats on the ends of the lines. Southeastern Indians would also poison river pools, using smashed buckeyes and other natural poisons. Choctaw Indians used one of the most innovative tactics, taking advantage of a catfish's tendency to feed by scent. They constructed cylindrical-shaped traps from fresh buffalo skins. Each trap was designed so a watching angler could shut it quickly with a string when catfish swam in to investigate the odor.

White men likewise were quick to discover the value of catfish as food fish and the bounties that Southern rivers offered. On big rivers, in fact, a commercial catfishing industry developed early in the 1800s.

Samuel Clemens (Mark Twain), who grew up less than 40 miles from the Mississippi River, offers a glimpse of the commercial fishing industry that obviously existed at the time in *The Adventures of Huckleberry Finn*, written in 1884 and set in the late 1840s. The passage refers to a catfish that Huckleberry Finn and Jim had caught on a setline: "He would a been worth a good deal over at the village. They peddle out such a fish as that by the pound in the market house there; everybody buys some of him; his meat's as white as snow and makes a good fry."

Farther up in the same passage, the description of the fish offers a hint of just how large a catfish sometimes showed up—or at least was reported to have shown up—from the Mississippi River: "Well, the days went along, and the river went down between its banks again; and about the first thing we done was to bait one of the big hooks with a skinned rabbit and set it and catch a cat-fish that was as big as a man, being six foot two inches long, and weighed over two hundred pounds."

Reports from the Lewis and Clark expedition also include mention of a large "white" catfish, 1½ meters in length from the Missouri River, and Capt. Bill Heckman, a longtime steamboat pilot and Missouri River historian, reported that catfish in the 125- to 200-pound range were common in the 1800s.

Adding credence to such reports is a letter sent in 1879 from Dr. J. G. W. Steedman, chairman of the Missouri Fish Commission, to Professor Spencer F. Baird, U.S. commissioner of Fish and Fisheries: "Your letter requesting shipment to you of a large Mississippi catfish was received this morning. Upon visiting our markets this afternoon, I luckily found two—one of 144 lbs., the other of 150 lbs. The latter I shipped to you by Express."

Whether because of navigational projects, which have channelized and pooled up most of the South's largest rivers, reduced water quality caused by industrialization, widespread commercial fishing, or some combination, none of those absolute giants have shown up for more than a century.

Even so, the historical accounts do give angler cause to wonder just how big a catfish still swims in the Missouri or Mississippi River. Plus, even recent years have produced numerous triple-digit-weight catfish from several major rivers, with some of those having been caught by sport fishermen.

Modern Sport

"All fish must be alive and will be released back into the Santee-Cooper Lakes."

That's Rule No. 1 for the National Championship Catfishing Tournament, held annually out of Randolph's Landing on South Carolina's Lake Marion.

The National Championship, a 20-year Santee Cooper tradition, offers a pretty good snapshot of how sport catfishing has developed in recent years. As late as the mid-1990s, the tournament didn't even have a catch-and-release category, and there was no limit on the number of fish that could be weighed. Teams of anglers brought in boatloads of catfish in hopes of amassing the heaviest total weight.

In 1997, the first year a catch-and-release category was added to the competition, participation was only modest. Most anglers didn't even know how to keep big catfish alive, and their focus was on the bigger-money total-weight category. In 1998, interest grew, and more than one-third of the total pounds brought to the scales were in the form of live fish.

The following year, with ever-expanding interest in the catch-and-release category, the tournament paid equal prizes for the top five places, dead or alive, and the top five places, catch-and-release. Catches could be entered in both categories, so anglers who kept their fish in good condition could potentially double their earnings. In 2000, the tournament went to a total catch-and-release format, with a 10-fish limit.

Nate Bristow, owner of Randolph's Landing and operator of the tournament for more than 10 years, has always considered it the fishermen's tournament. Participating anglers determine rule changes for the following year, he emphasizes. He only recommends changes based on talk he hears among anglers and on what seems best for the tournament and for the resources.

Therefore, the quick and radical turn toward conservation in the National Championship, which attracts catfishermen from all over the country, reflects a respect for catfish and catfishing, which has been growing gradually for several years.

Several regional catfishing tournament circuits now operate on a catch-and-release-only basis, and many have limits of only three to five fish so anglers can take the best possible care of the fish. Many catfish guides, meanwhile, require or recommend that clients return all large cats to the water, and many other anglers only keep smaller fish for table fare.

In several states that border the Missouri River, commercial catfishing was banned in the mid-1990s to protect the valuable and extremely popular sport-fishery that catfish now provide on the big river. Local anglers contend that fishing has improved dramatically

Figure 1. Catch-and-release has become much more popular among catfishermen in recent years. George Logan, a dedicated flathead fisherman from Winston-Salem, North Carolina, releases all the catfish he catches.

since the change, and some expect an eventual return of the giant catfish of old.

Meanwhile, on other waterways where sport catfishing has become very popular, lawmakers are being encouraged to give commercial catfishing regulations a harder look. Anglers question why public fisheries can be sold, often virtually unregulated, for private gain. They also point toward the higher total economic value of large catfish as a recreational resource.

Looking beyond the conservation picture, the development of catfishing as serious sport is evidenced by the ever-increasing number of catfish guides on waterways throughout the South. On Santee Cooper alone, dozens of guides fish exclusively, or at least extensively, for trophy catfish.

Tackle industry trends also reveal the growing popularity of sport-catfishing. A decade ago, no tackle was marketed to catfishermen, except for stinkbaits and a few prefabricated trotlines. Today, several manufacturers offer high-quality catfishing rods, reels, and rod/reel combinations. There are even hooks and lines designed specifically with the needs of catfishermen in mind.

While trophy catfish understandably attract the lion's share of the headlines, fishing for smaller channel and blue catfish also has become extremely popular in recent years, especially in small waters that offer good public bank-fishing access. Throughout the South, small lakes owned by state game departments and other government entities are stocked regularly with catfish to provide opportunities for family recreation.

Fisheries managers like catfish because they are easy to grow in hatcheries, and they don't require additional management steps after they are stocked. Fishermen like cats in small lakes because they are generally easy to catch, and they fight hard for their size.

I know that in my own home, almost nothing I can announce will bring quicker or broader smiles to my own kids' faces than "We're going to the catfish pond."

The pond we like to visit is a small kids-only fishing pond operated by the Georgia Wildlife Resources Division where cat densities are kept high. A piece of hot dog cast out on a split shot rig rarely even finds bottom before the line races off.

As more families discover catfishing, whether from the banks of a small lake or with a guide for big cats on a major river, the popularity of the sport promises to continue growing. Meanwhile, as catfishermen and their tackle become ever more serious and refined, catfish records are likely to continue falling.

Whether anyone will ever land one quite like Huck Finn and Jim did, only time will tell. In the meantime, it doesn't hurt to dream about it.

Chapter 1

Major Species

Flathead Catfish

A bulldog in catfish's clothing, a flathead is a different kind of cat. Shattering catfish stereotypes and stout rods, plus fishermen's hearts on occasion, flatheads thrive on live meals, usually of fish. Favorite haunts of flatheads are inseparably linked to structure, cover, and river channel edges, so locating them is a science in itself. To many anglers, even veteran catfishermen, flatheads present a mystery. They are tough customers, and catching them consistently requires a well-planned approach.

As the name suggests, a flathead's most distinguishing feature is its broad, flat head, which comes complete with a big mouth and a bit of an underbite. Most flatheads are thick in the body, but without the big bellies that hefty blues often grow. They have squared-off tails.

Flathead coloration varies markedly from fish to fish, even within a given river or lake. A mustardy yellow provides the backdrop for most flatheads' markings, explaining the popular nickname of yellow cat. However, some flatheads are mostly brown or close to a milky white. Almost all flatheads have mottling of darker colors, hence another common nickname of appaloosa cat. On many fish, the markings are muted.

Big-river fish by nature, flatheads are native to all the major river systems that drain into the Mississippi, Mobile, and Rio Grande river systems. Some of the South's finest fisheries, however, exist along river systems where the species is not indigenous. As examples, Occoquan Reservoir in Virginia, the Santee Cooper Lakes in South Carolina, and numerous coastal rivers from Virginia to Georgia serve up world-class flathead fishing.

In some of those waters, the fish were formally introduced by biologists, primarily during the 1950s and 1960s, at a time when attitudes about trying new species in waterways were largely carefree. In other cases, anglers who had their own management plans transferred the flatheads. In a few cases, the fish found their way into systems by unknown means. Flatheads are highly adaptable fish, and several major populations have begun with only a few fish.

Non-native flathead fisheries have stirred up a fair amount of controversy, especially around tidal rivers along the south Atlantic coast in which the big cats have been accused of gobbling up historically popular redbreast sunfish populations and ruining the fishing. Eradication efforts have even been attempted on some rivers, with minimal success. Flathead reduction efforts have achieved some success; however, flatheads are in these systems to stay, and anglers are slowly beginning to embrace the exciting fisheries that have developed.

The world-record flathead catfish, caught in Kansas in 1998, weighed an amazing 123 pounds. The top flatheads on record from most southern states exceed the 70-pound mark, and a few fish have come quite close to triple-digit weights. The Texas state record, a former world record, weighed 98½ pounds.

Numerous flatheads weighing more than 100 pounds have been caught by commercial anglers over the years from big rivers like the Arkansas, Missouri, Tennessee, and Mississippi. During recent years some giant flatheads, which have less commercial value than small to medium-sized fish, have been released.

Catfishermen remain divided as to whether flatheads or blues deserve the title as America's biggest catfish, and each camp has a legitimate argument. Historic top-end commercial catches definitely favor blues, showing the species' amazing growth potential.

However, the size of the current all-tackle world record for each species places flatheads as the top cats.

In most rivers or lakes where flatheads thrive, a 20-pound flathead catfish is only a decent catch. Fishermen commonly catch 30-pound-plus fish. Many fishermen consider 40 pounds the trophy-flathead benchmark, like a 3-pound crappie or a 10-pound large-mouth bass.

Anglers rarely catch large flatheads by accident, and they almost never catch one by spreading out chicken livers or stinkbait on the bottom. Most adult flatheads that do get hooked incidentally take live shiners or shad that are dangled for largemouth bass or striped bass. Of course, hooking a big flathead and catching a big flathead are two very different things, and a largemouth fisherman who hooks one of these giants typically ends up with a story about a "big one that got away."

Throughout the South, a fraternity of flathead specialists has been unlocking the secrets of these large and powerful cats over the past couple of decades. Only a small amount of scientific information exists concerning flathead behavior, so it has been left up to the anglers to figure out the fish's habits and haunts and to find out what makes them bite.

Conquering these king-sized cats begins with identifying their holding grounds. Flathead specialists will commonly spend an hour or more searching for fish with electronics before they ever put a line down. In fact, serious river fishermen will sometimes search for several hours during the afternoon, scouting for a full night of fishing.

River fishermen study big holes along outside bends, looking both for fish and for the cover that holds them. In reservoirs, they search over structural features all along the inundated river channel. Flatheads remain river fish, even in reservoirs, and rarely stray far from inundated channels.

Once fish are found or an angler settles upon a hole that is likely to produce, attractive live-bait offerings must be properly presented. As far as bait types are concerned, live bream top the popularity charts. Other outstanding flathead offerings for certain waters include live gizzard shad, bullhead catfish, eels, perch, and carp.

Figure 2. The author and Santee Cooper guide Don Drose hoist a couple of hefty flatheads, caught during the fall over the inundated Santee River channel on Lake Marion. Flatheads rarely stray far from major creek and river channels, even in reservoirs.

The best bait to use depends on a number of factors, among them the flatheads' normal diet in a waterway, what a fisherman can attain, and what is legal to use as bait in a state. While flatheads are opportunistic predators that occasionally will eat just about any kind of live fish, they seemingly favor the types of fish they are accustomed to seeing and eating.

Flathead fishermen typically dangle their baits just off the bottom. In reservoirs, this can usually be accomplished by simply dropping down-lines to the bottom, setting each rod in a holder, and cranking each reel a turn or two. Rivers, with their currents and often dense cover, sometimes call for more creative rigs.

Once the baits are down, flathead fishing becomes a waiting game. It's not unusual for a group of flatheads, all clearly visible on a graph, to lie with half a dozen lively baits around them for an hour before one suddenly decides to strike. Then, before an angler has time to pry that rod out of its holder, one or more other rods will surge violently downward. For that reason, flathead fishermen often will stay in a spot for a couple of hours even without a single bite.

Of course, the true challenge begins the moment a big flathead decides to bite. On the line, flatheads fight like champion boxers, with strong jabs and incredible endurance. They waste no energy on useless flash or fast runs. They just hold deep as long as possible, lunging repeatedly. Big flatheads will immediately head for cover upon feeling a hook. If they reach it, the fight usually ends early, with the catfish remaining champ and the fisherman wondering what hit him.

Because of the size and strength of flatheads, anglers who go after them typically do so with heavy gear. Lines commonly used range from 30-pound-test monofilament to 130-pound-test braided line. Popular hook sizes range from 3/O to 8/O, with bait size being the major determining factor. Weights range from an ounce to about 8 ounces.

Medium-sized conventional reels that hold a lot of line and have a low gear ratio are the norm for this style of fishing, and they must be matched with stout rods that have a lot of backbone. Quality rod holders, a good graph, and a large net also border on being essential equipment for serious flathead fishing.

Of the major catfish species, flatheads are easily the most nocturnal, so many flathead specialists do the bulk of their fishing at night. Many will scout through the afternoon and set up around dusk. Lake and reservoir anglers may move several times during the night, but river fishermen often set up in one spot and stay there until morning.

Fall is prime time for catching reservoir flatheads. The fish stack up in holes along old river channels, so finding good groups of fish to set up on becomes more practical. Spring is the next best time, with summer sometimes tough and midwinter fishing almost useless. In rivers, fishing typically remains good throughout the warm months, except during early summer, when the flatheads spawn.

During the spawn, a different breed of angler partakes in a totally different style of flathead fishing. "Grappling" or "noodling" refers to wading along the edge of a river, reaching into holes in bluff banks, which are where the big catfish spawn, and wrestling out 30-, 40-, and 50-pound flatheads by hand.

Whether they are landed by hand or by rod-and-reel, flathead catfish put anglers to the ultimate catfishing test.

Blue Catfish

Screaming initial runs are the hallmark of hefty blue catfish. They grab baits on the move, wasting no time with noncommittal nibbles, and they don't slow down until the issue is forced. That is, *if* anyone is able to force the issue. More than a few blues have stripped reels of all their line without ever slowing. Blue catfish don't have quite the tenacity of flatheads in their fight, but big blues are definitely prime candidates to yank a rod from the hands of any angler caught unaware.

Blue catfish grow to massive proportions. The world-record blue, caught in 2001 from the Arkansas portion of the Mississippi River, weighed 116 pounds, 12 ounces, and line-class world records include more than a dozen fish that weighed more than 75 pounds.

However, historical commercial catches suggest that the biggest blue catfish on the sport-fishing record represents only a shadow of the blue catfish's top-end potential. Albeit many years ago, cats of more than twice the size of the world-record blue catfish allegedly have been pulled from big rivers like the Missouri and the Mississippi by commercial fishermen.

The blue catfish world record was broken three times during the 1990s and again in 2001, and most serious catfishermen believe it will fall several more times as increasing numbers of anglers

Figure 3. Charles Ashley of Marion, Arkansas, used Spam to catch the world-record blue catfish. The giant cat, which weighed 116 pounds, 12 ounces, came from the West Memphis area of the Mississippi River in summer 2001. Photo courtesy of the Arkansas Game and Fish Commission.

become ever more serious about the pursuit of these giant fish and become better equipped to tangle with them. How high the record will go, no one really knows.

Looking at state-record blues from the South, the 1990s produced new record fish in Alabama, Arkansas, Florida, Kentucky,

Louisiana, Mississippi, Missouri, North Carolina, South Carolina, Tennessee, Texas, and Virginia. Nine of those fish weighed more than 90 pounds. Six reached triple-digit weights. Plus, the Arkansas record fell again with the new world-record blue catfish.

As their name suggests, blue catfish are generally blue to bluish gray. However, some take on a more neutral coloration and look a lot like giant channel catfish. In waters where both species exist and grow to large sizes, the only certain way to distinguish one from the other is to count rays on the anal fin. Blues have 30 or more rays. Channels have less. The profiles of most jumbo-sized blues leave no secrets about their fondness for eating. Any blue that weighs more than about 45 pounds is apt to have a huge belly.

Blue catfish are big-river fish by nature. Their native range in the South includes the biggest rivers in the Mississippi River drainage and Gulf coast, including the Arkansas, Missouri, Ohio, Tennessee, and Red River systems. Like flatheads, however, blues have been stocked in reservoirs throughout the South and into many river systems that they are not indigenous to.

The best concentrations of the largest fish still exist primarily in the South's biggest rivers. Most other waterways that support excellent populations of big blues—among them Santee Cooper, several large Texas reservoirs, and various rivers along the Atlantic coast—have the common denominator of extensive and usually diverse forage.

Blue catfish are also regularly stocked in many smaller reservoirs. While the blues rarely grow to super sizes in small waters, they generally perform well, providing a good fishing opportunity, and they commonly reach 20 or 30 pounds. Blues are often stocked in addition to channel catfish in these types of waters, adding the bonus possibility of a trophy fish for anglers.

One thing that has brought blue catfish extra popularity over the past couple of decades, as anglers have grown ever more dedicated to catfishing, is their willingness to bite 12 months of the year. On many southern rivers and lakes, fishermen follow blues through the seasons, adapting their strategies according to conditions but never hanging up their gear for the season.

In fact, some blue catfish specialists like the cold months best. Winter conditions limit the comfort zones of blue catfish and the baitfish they feed on, forcing the fish and their favorite foods to pile up in predictable locations. Deep river holes and the deep waters near the dams of reservoirs often hold outstanding concentrations of blue catfish through the winter.

Blue cats roam far more than other catfish species do. They follow schools of shad and herring through the open waters of reservoirs and from one hole to another in rivers. While blues do relate to structural features, like channel edges, humps, and points, food dictates where they will hold, more so than any other single factor.

Baitfish typically dominate the diets of large blue catfish, but various mollusk species also provide important forage in many waterways. Even where baitfish abound, blues may feed primarily to mussels at certain times. During early spring, for example, blues sometimes move very shallow because shallow flats offer warmer water temperatures. Those same flats are commonly covered with mussels, which the cats feast upon.

More so than other species of catfish, blue catfish like current. Even in reservoirs, they feed best when water is being pulled through hydroelectric dams, creating current. In tailwaters, the water being "on" or "off" tends to dictate whether the blue cat bite will be on or off. On free-flowing rivers, water levels dictate which holes the blues will use or where in a given hole they will feed. Blue cats that lie in very slack water tend to be resting fish that are not very likely to take a bait.

Like most catfish, blues are somewhat nocturnal. They feed well day and night, however, and some fishermen consistently do better under the sun than the moon. The biggest difference in the big cats' behavior after hours is that they tend to stray into shallower water.

Day or night, the most popular way to fish for blue catfish is to lay out lines rigged with cut bait on the bottom. In reservoirs, anglers often set up along the slope on the side of a hump or the edge of a channel. That way, they can spread lines on both sides of the boat and cover a range of depths.

In rivers, the best approach often is to anchor upstream of a hole and cast down into it. Because of powerful currents that characterize really large rivers, fishermen often need several ounces of weight on their lines, which they typically rig Carolina style.

In tailwaters, boating anglers often use three-way rigs for blues. Many tailwaters have very rocky bottoms, and baits laid out on the bottom will soon be hung in the rocks. A three-way rig, which has a weight on the bottom and a hook on a dropper line, up from the weight, allows a bait to be fished very near the bottom but not quite on it. Fishermen hold boats as steady as they can in the current, and each angler keeps his rod in hand, reeling and releasing line as needed to keep the weight ticking the bottom but not laying on it.

Drifting, which can be done in several different ways, also ranks among the most popular approaches for blue catfish. Drifting allows anglers to cover a lot of water, which makes it a very effective approach when baitfish and catfish are spread out. Drifting also allows fishermen to find the most active cats, instead of waiting for the cats to find them.

Small blues will hit a lot of different kinds of baits, and fishermen catch them consistently on many of the same baits that produce the best action from channel catfish. In fact, small blues and channels are commonly caught together in lakes and rivers where the species coexist. As they gain pounds and convert more to a diet of baitfish, however, blue catfish become much more prone to grab an offering of cut fish than other kinds of bait.

The No. 1 bait for a big blue catfish, most veteran big-cat anglers would agree, is a big chunk of fresh skipjack herring. Very oily baitfish, skipjack are the food of choice for big blues and the bait of choice of any angler who can catch enough skipjack for a day of fishing. Other popular baitfish species in various places include threadfin and gizzard shad, blueback herring, and alewives. Although its use is not widespread in the South, another extremely effective type of bait for blue catfish is coagulated blood.

Whether they drift with blood, lay out chunks of skipjack, or dangle threadfin shad just off the bottom, anglers who target big blues need to go out loaded for bear. Powerful currents and fish that can grow to triple-digit weights demand rods and reels that have plenty of pulling power and heavy, abrasion-resistant line.

Any time a reel's clicker starts screaming for help in blue catfish waters, the fish at the other end of the line might the one that would rewrite the record books. At that point, the only question that remains is whether the angler at the other end and the gear in-between have what it takes to bring that fish to the boat.

Channel Catfish

While overgrown blue and flathead catfish attract most of the catfishing headlines, channel cats are the whiskered fish that most southern anglers know and love. Channel catfish abound in streams and lakes both big and small throughout the South, and virtually everyone who has ever fished in this part of the country has done battle with a channel cat or two.

While channels never reach triple-digit weights, they do grow plenty large to provide outstanding sport. Plus, where there is one channel cat, there usually are several. The 1- to 5-pound fish that abound in most rivers and lakes fight great on light to medium-sized tackle, and fish up to about 10 pounds show up on occasion virtually everywhere channel catfish swim. In some waterways, primarily major rivers and impoundments along them, some channel cats grow to heavyweight proportions.

The world-record channel catfish came from South Carolina's Santee Cooper Lakes, which, ironically, are far better known for the giant blues and flatheads they produce than for big channels. In 1964, when W. B. Waley caught the 58-pound giant that still tops the list of channels ever landed, the other two species had not yet even been introduced to Santee Cooper.

Looking past the all-tackle world record, all 18 line-class world-record channel catfish listed in *Official World and USA State Fresh Water Angling Records* (2002) were established with fish that weighed more than 20 pounds. Half weighed more than 30 pounds, and four broke the 40-pound barrier.

Looking at state-record channel catfish from the South, all southern states list a state-record channel cat, and the smallest of those, which came from West Virginia, still weighed an impressive 21.25 pounds. Seven southern states list a state-record channel catfish of 40 pounds or more.

Channel catfish are often called speckled cats because they have small black "speckles" on their backs and sides when they are young. The markings fade as the cats grow. Channels range from slate blue to brown on their backs. The color fades to gray or tan on the fish's sides and white on their bellies. Their tails are deeply forked. They are lean and mean compared to their larger cousins, lacking the bulldog thickness of flatheads or the potbellies of heavyweight blues.

Because of their color, fin configurations, and tail shape, channel catfish are commonly confused with white catfish and small blue catfish in waters where the species coexist. While the difference is sometimes apparent, the most certain way to distinguish among species is to count the rays on a fish's anal fin. White cats have fewer than 24 rays. Blue cats have more than 30 rays. If the count falls in between, the fish is a channel catfish.

Channel catfish are very well distributed throughout the South. However, they are not native to most river systems that drain toward the Atlantic Ocean. These waters were once the domains of white catfish and bullheads only. In addition to waters where they naturally occur, channels are stocked extensively in private, pay-per-day fishing ponds and in public fishing lakes.

The widespread abundance of channel catfish in all types of waters reflects the fact that they are true generalists, in terms of both habitat and diet. They do well in vast, powerful rivers, small farm ponds, and everything in-between. They also make use of a huge range of habitat types, among them riprap banks, brushpiles, flats, river holes, dams, and rocky points.

As for food, channel catfish eat a little bit of everything, and dominant forage really depends on what's available in a waterway. Broadly speaking, they eat a lot of invertebrates, including aquatic and terrestrial insects, annelids, various mollusks, and crustaceans, plus some small vertebrates, especially fish.

As channel cats grow larger, they do tend to turn increasingly to larger menu items. Stomach-sample studies done on catfish from the Missouri River and Santee Cooper, where large channel catfish were abundant, showed that the biggest channels in both waterways ate mostly small fish.

Figure 4. Jackie Vancleave, a guide on Tennessee's Reelfoot Lake, admires a nice channel catfish. Channels, which abound in rivers and lakes of all sizes throughout the South, are the cats that most Southerners are best acquainted with.

Channel catfish growth rates vary enormously from one water-way to the next, with no apparent geographic correlations. Some of the world's fastest-growing channel catfish that have been identi-fied are in Canada's Red River. Other fast-growing populations have been documented in the Deep South. Research results suggest that the most significant factors affecting growth rates are forage makeup and channel catfish density. Where channel cat numbers are extremely high, competition for preferred foods seems to keep growth rates relatively low.

Like other kinds of cats, channels spawn between spring and early summer. Spawning activity may start as early as March in the Deep South, but most spawning occurs during May and June through most of the region. Channels, which begin spawning at four or five years of age, prefer secluded, semidarkened areas with protection from the current and some visual cover. Clusters of woody debris, root balls, bank burrows, and spaces between rocks all provide good spawning habitat.

Very generally speaking, channel catfish tend to move up tributaries, away from main river channels and reservoir bodies when they spawn, and concentrations tend to be highest up creeks during spring and early summer. As summer progresses and then gives way to fall and winter, more channels will be found back down in the big water.

As already noted, though, channel catfish are generalists to the highest degree. At almost any given time, there will be some channels piled up on main-lake humps, others hiding around laydowns in tributaries, and still others cruising rocky ledges up a major river. The best areas for channel catfish, whether up a tributary or way down a lake, have a wide range of depths and habitat offerings in a single area.

Waters above and below dams, bridge crossings, long points that stretch close to major creek or river channels, and classic river holes on outside bends are all good areas to find concentrations of channel catfish. Within those areas, fishermen should test a range of depths and cover types and waters both in and out of any current until they figure out where the cats are piled up.

Through much of the year, channels will hold deep in holes or deep in dense cover through the day. They'll feed readily if food is laid in front of them during the day, but they won't go out of their way looking for meals. At night, they will move shallower and feed much more actively. During the cool months, the fish will stay in the deep holes all day but will feed just as well during the day as they will through the night.

The best bait to use for channel catfish could be the subject of quite a debate among veteran catfishermen. Various commercially manufactured dip baits would be well represented in the discussion, especially around rivers. Good dips work wonderfully anywhere there is enough current to wash their scent downstream.

Various natural offerings would also get their share of votes. In waters where the cats eat a lot of fish, many veteran anglers prefer small shad or herring (or small pieces of the same) over all other offerings. In rocky streams, meanwhile, it's tough to beat freshly caught crawfish or hellgrammites.

In terms of overall appeal under a broad range of conditions, chicken livers or blood bait might get the nod. Since livers are available at any grocery store and are easy to fish with, they easily would win the popularity contest over blood.

Tactics and tackle for channel catfish may be even more diverse than bait selections because of the diversity of channel catfish waters and variances in the size of cats that anglers are apt to encounter. In a small pond, for example, a light spincasting outfit spooled with 10-pound test and rigged with a small treble hook and rubber-core sinker would be just right for the task. The same setup simply wouldn't do the job on a big river, where currents push hard and 10-pound-plus channels share waters with heavyweight flatheads and blues.

Among the most common approaches to fishing for channel catfish is to spread several offerings around an anchored boat or out from a spot along the shore. Many anglers favor Carolina rigs, using an egg weight of approximately 1 ounce. Where current or bottom slope would cause egg weights to roll, some anglers substitute bell sinkers.

In tailwaters or other places where current and rocks or other snags along the bottom won't allow spreading baits, many anglers like to drift over likely holding areas and fish three-way rigs vertically. Again, the amount of weight needed, the best size of line, and the type of tackle all vary dramatically from place to place. Still, in other places, a float rig or bottom-bumping drift rig is better suited for the job.

The generalist behavior of channel catfish is both good and bad for fishermen. The good part is that channels can be caught in so many different waterways and types of areas. The bad part is that it is very difficult to pinpoint anything even close to a formula for finding and catching the most channel catfish.

Bullhead Catfish

The ugly ducklings of the catfish clan, bullheads get overshadowed by other species of cats through most of the South. Some waterways have abundant bullheads, but unless a river, lake, or pond does not produce channels or other catfish as well, bullheads don't attract much attention from fishermen. While typically cooperative and fun to catch, bullheads simply get beat out by bigger, stronger cats in the South.

Three different bullhead species—brown bullheads, black bullheads, and yellow bullheads—call southern waters home and grow large enough to attract at least a bit of angling attention. Brown bullheads are the most abundant overall; yellow bullheads are the most broadly distributed.

All three popular bullhead species are similar in feeding habits and habitat preferences, with slight variances in the latter. Brown bullheads are found in larger waterways on average than the other species, and yellow bullheads are a bit more likely than their cousins to be in clear, flowing water. Black bullheads may inhabit the smallest, murkiest ponds around.

None of the bullheads grow terribly large. The biggest bullhead in the record books from anywhere in the country is an 8-pound, 15-ounce black bullhead, which was caught in Michigan. The world-record brown bullhead, which weighed 6 pounds, 2 ounces and was caught by Bobby L. Gibson Jr. from the Pearl River in Mississippi, is the biggest bullhead on record from the South. The world-record yellow bullhead, which came from Arizona, weighed 4 pounds, 8 ounces.

Figure 5. While bullheads don't grow as large as other kinds of cats, they are willing biters that often provide fast action in ponds and creeks.

Bullheads eat a little bit of everything. They definitely scavenge for some of their food, but they also eat a fair number of small living critters. A bullhead's diet might include worms, leeches, aquatic insects, small fish, freshwater shrimp, fish eggs, various mollusks, and even vegetation, among other things.

Bullheads are stubby little fish that average between half a pound and a couple of pounds, depending on the species and the location. They have fat "bullish" heads, as the name suggests, and square tails. Most have mottled skin.

No bullhead would win a tug-of-war. They are generally very willing customers, however, and where there is one, there are usually several more. For that reason, they make great targets for kids or other newcomers to fishing.

They are also known to have very tasty meat, which adds to their popularity in certain places with fishermen who want catfish to take home. Fillets aren't big, but it is not usually difficult to catch a good mess of fish, and fishing pressure is unlikely to dent any populations of these prolific spawners.

Another positive attribute of bullheads is that they can survive where other cats cannot, providing additional opportunities for some catfishermen. Bullheads tolerate turbid waters with low dissolved-oxygen levels, and they are not fussy about their food. They can live in just about any pond that supports any kind of life.

However, they don't compete well against larger catfish species, and flatheads think they are candy.

One downside of fishing for bullheads with youngsters is that these little cats have super-sharp dorsal and pectoral fins. The bullheads' small size makes them a little tougher than larger fish to grab without getting poked. Having been jabbed by one when I was a kid, I can attest that it really hurts and that it can get infected.

Catching bullheads calls for no special techniques or tackle. In fact, in the small waters where these fish are most abundant, fishermen generally don't even need to search for the fish. The bullheads will find the bait. They are usually widespread along the edges of ponds and are always on the lookout for a meal.

Most bullhead fishermen pick spots to set up based on where there is a grassy bank that looks nice to sit on or a tree hanging over providing shade, more so than where they expect the bullheads to be. They just plop down in a spot, cast their offerings out and wait on a bite, rarely having to wait for long. If the bullheads don't cooperate fairly quickly in a waterway that is known to hold them in decent numbers, the best bet is to move a good distance down the bank and try again.

One of the best baits for bullheads comes right out of the home refrigerator. They cannot resist slices of hot dogs, which are also cheap and neat to fish with and stay on the hook fairly well. Other effective baits for bullheads include cheese, worms, bacon, chicken livers, and commercial catfish baits.

Whatever the bait choice, most bullhead fishermen keep their rigs very simple, using a No. 2 to No. 6 hook and just enough weight to make casting practical and to carry the bait to the bottom. Rods and reels can be equally simple. Any spinning or spincasting outfit will do the job, and more than a few bullheads have been caught on cane poles. Light tackle and 6- or 8-pound test line add a little extra fighting fun after bullheads are hooked.

The only skill that newcomers to bullhead fishing really need to master is that of grabbing the rod quickly to set the hook. Bullheads rarely pick at their food. They suck it in, and any angler who doesn't react quickly will have to remove the hook from far down in the fish.

For this reason, and for the sake of the fish's sharp spines, needle-nose pliers ought to be included in any list of bullhead fishing gear.

White Catfish

Despite being the largest of the original cats in South Atlantic river systems, white catfish are in some ways the South's forgotten cats. In addition to having had three species of larger and more glamorous catfish stocked through much of their native range, white cats suffer from a major identity crisis.

For starters, white catfish are not white, excepting their bellies and chin barbels. Instead, they are gray to tan and sometimes mottled. Their backs have a bluish tint (much like blue catfish), which leads to the second aspect of their identity crisis. Since channel or blue catfish now reside in many of the same rivers and lakes where white catfish are found, anglers misidentify most white cats that they catch as one of the two better-known species.

White catfish are generally a bit stouter than channels or blues. Their tails are also a little less deeply forked, and there are slight distinctions in fin shapes. However, those distinctions would be tough to pick out easily with a single fish in hand. The most distinctive feature is that white cats always have fewer than 24 rays on their anal fin. Channels and blues have more.

Adding even more confusion, while white catfish look like small channels or blues, they are actually more closely related to bullheads than to the larger cats. In fact, white catfish used to be included in the genus *Ictalurus*, along with channels and blues, but in the late 1980s, fisheries scientists officially moved them to the genus *Ameiurus*, which includes all the bullheads.

White catfish are native to Atlantic coastal rivers from the northeastern United States all the way to Florida and to most rivers that drain into the Gulf of Mexico in Florida and Alabama. They have been stocked in ponds and lakes in other parts of the country, but not significantly through the South. Half a dozen southern states list a state record for white catfish, all within the species' native range.

The world-record white catfish, a 22-pound giant, came from California, where the species is not native. The biggest white cat on record from the South came from Florida's Withlacoochee River, which drains into the Gulf of Mexico. It weighed in at an impressive 18.88 pounds.

The best white catfish fishing overall is found through the lower reaches of coastal rivers. They don't like swift current, and they can tolerate more turbidity, warmer temperatures, and higher salinity than other freshwater catfish species. In fact, fishing for white cats can be good in brackish water all the way down into the sounds.

White cats also do well in impoundments along rivers within their range. However, they share most impoundments with channel catfish, which attract more attention from fishermen. Most fishermen never make any distinction if they are catching cats of both species (or even if they're catching all whites, in many instances).

White catfish spawn in shallow water, near the bank, over sand or gravel, sometimes around some kind of cover. The male runs the female off once the eggs are laid and protects the eggs and the fry. White cats grow very slowly. Even in the South, a 1-pound fish is likely to be four or five years old. Small fish, various crustaceans, and aquatic insects are the mainstay food sources of white cats. They are omnivorous and somewhat opportunistic, however, and eat a little bit of everything on occasion.

Like their cousins, the bullheads, white cats are quite cooperative. They make good targets for family outings because they feed more readily through the day than do most other kinds of catfish. They also tend to hang out in groups, so fast action is the norm once anglers locate fish. They typically bite aggressively, and they fight well for their size.

In coastal rivers, where white catfish are most likely to be the dominant catfish species, they feed heavily on various shad and herring species that move up and down those rivers. Small shad are also important forage for whites in many southern impoundments. For that reason, fresh shad or herring are tough to beat as bait. Shrimp offer a good alternative when baitfish aren't readily available, as do good old-fashioned earthworms.

Most baitfish need to be cut into strips. White catfish average only a pound or two, so small pieces of bait will attract far more bites than big chunks. An adult American shad or blueback herring probably has enough meat on it for a whole day of fishing for white cats. Very small baitfish can be fished whole. It makes no difference whether shad or herring are dead or alive, but fresh is always better than frozen.

If currents are minimal and a river is somewhat stable, white cats often will be out in the channel in big groups. If the river is up, they will move to sluggish backwater areas. Either way, they like a sand or gravel bottom, which they will stay close to. In lakes and reservoirs, tops of points, flats, and sandbars near creek channels stand out as good areas to look for white cats.

Fishing for white catfish calls for no special gear or tactics. Light to medium-sized spinning gear, 10- or 12-pound test line, enough weight to keep the bait on the bottom, and a No. 2 or No. 4 hook will do the job. Circle hooks are nice for white catfish because they generally hook fish in the corner of the mouth, and small cats, which have small mouths, can be difficult to unhook when they really slurp baits down.

While white catfish aren't white, they do have white meat. I haven't eaten white cats (unless someone thought some were channels and I never knew otherwise), but their meat is reported to be firm and delicious.

Chapter 2

Catfish Waters

Creeks and Rivers

Through a hard turn, an otherwise lively creek slows to a crawl. Its waters, which average less than knee deep, pool up in an outside-bend hole that would float a man's hat. A dirt bank rises sharply along the edge of the pool, having been sculpted sheer by countless flood-level flows. The same eroding waters have toppled a couple of trees. The fallen trees now stretch into the creek, their tops resting on the pool's bottom.

Among the treetops, in the deepest, darkest part of the pool, lurks a channel catfish of 5 pounds or so. Half a dozen smaller cats set among the branches, also tight to the bottom. They look docile—almost dead, in fact—but any misguided critter drifting down among the branches would quickly cause any such notion to be dispelled.

A couple hundred miles downstream, in a river to which this creek is a tributary of a tributary of a tributary of a tributary, a hard turn in the big river's direction also creates a fine catfish hole. The hole this riverbend forms is 80 feet deep, instead of 8 feet, and its outside bend is close to one-eighth of a mile long. Dozens of trees litter the hole's bottom, and among them lie literally hundreds of cats. A few are well over 50 pounds.

In some ways, these two holes are vastly different, and fishing each would call for completely different tackle and tactics. The distinctions all have to do with scale, however, and in a sense the holes are much alike. Both are formed by big channel bends, and catfish relate to both in much the same way.

Whether tumbling or tidal, minuscule or massive, wooded or urbanized, streams go hand-in-hand with catfish. River fish by nature, cats abound in moving waters throughout the South. Excepting mountain streams, which are too cold and swift to support many (or in some cases, any) cats, catfish of some variety are found in virtually all creeks and river systems in the South. Even brackish waters along the Atlantic and eastern Gulf coasts support good populations of white catfish.

Generally speaking, small streams support channel and/or bullhead catfish and, in some cases, white catfish. As creeks begin joining forces to form more formidable flows, flatheads begin showing up, both within their native range and in numerous river systems where the species has been introduced. As rivers grow larger, so do the catfish they support, and flatheads commonly become more prevalent.

Blue catfish, more so than any of their cousins, are big-river fish. While exceptions exist, most blues are confined to large rivers and the lower reaches of medium-sized flows. Blues become the dominant cats in the lower portions of the South's biggest rivers.

In streams of all sizes and for all major catfish species, moving waters create a couple of significant advantages for fishermen. First, the current carries downstream scents emitted by bait, allowing anglers to attract fish from notably farther away than they could given still-water conditions. More significantly, the current tends to concentrate the fish and make their locations very predictable.

Cats like a big range of depths in an area and plenty of cover to relate to. They also like an area that has current pushing through it. However, that current must be moderated, and ideally it should broken in places or switch directions around an eddy. With a big range of habitat offerings in a small area, catfish can move quickly

Figure 6. Catfish are river fish by nature, and the biggest rivers, generally speaking, produce the biggest numbers of large catfish.

as conditions change. They can spend summer days deep in cover and move onto flats to feed at night. Likewise, they can find current to relate to even when rivers run low, but also have structure to hide behind when the same rivers rage.

In rivers of all sizes, major riverbends almost always rank among the best places to look for catfish. Holes that form on outside bends usually have slack currents beside stronger currents, deep water close to shallow bars, timber felled by bank erosion and in some cases, big swirling eddies. Riverbends are also elementary to identify, making them great starting points for fishing unfamiliar rivers.

Holes that form downstream of shoals, whether the shoals are exposed rapids or simply swift narrow river sections, also tend to hold a lot of cats. The shoals hold abundant food, generally speaking, and the cats often hold in the deep water right at the heads of pools, waiting for various foodstuff to get washed their way.

Mouths of tributaries also warrant checking out. Often a good hole forms where streams join forces, and the cats will set close to the confluence. If a creek mouth produces action and the creek is big enough to go up, it's also worth fishing the first few interesting-looking holes within the creek before moving on.

Where rivers are dammed, whether by low-head dams, lock-and-dam structures, or major hydroelectric dams, the tailwater portions below the dams almost always hold catfish. Every dam is different, and many can vary radically from day to day according to power-generation operations, but cats typically hold in deep water, often over rocks, where moderate currents run next to much stronger currents.

Wing dams or wing dikes, prevalent on many big rivers, likewise give cats all the conditions they prefer in small areas. Constructed of piled-up rocks, they provide good cover, and they funnel the river's flow to create unusual currents. Fish may be upstream or downstream of wing dikes or in the waters just out from them, depending on season and river level.

Riprap banks on rivers big and small have similar offerings, especially when they border deep runs and have good current flowing along them. Cats of all kinds will relate to riprap banks, which are often around bridges, downstream of dams, or bordering riverfront home sites.

In streams that don't have many well-defined holes or other distinctive features, fallen trees typically offer good holding areas for catfish. Trees that have been in the water for a long time, especially, tend to have scour holes around them, and their branches provide both cover and shade for catfish. Trees also tend to harbor a lot of critters that catfish feed on. Clusters of trees are best, but even isolated trees often will have a few cats in their branches. By moving from tree to tree, anglers often can catch a bunch of cats in a day without ever setting up on any one big hole where the cats are piled up.

Regarding the best baits for cats in creeks and rivers, most anglers come from one of two major schools of thought. One suggests that river cats are in their most natural environment and that the best way to catch the fish is with the same foods the catfish normally dine on. The other popular approach is to take advantage of the current and use offerings that emit a lot of odor.

The best natural baits vary enormously according to the size and character of the stream and according to the kind of catfish an angler hopes to catch. Hellgrammites are great bets in small rocky streams. Mollusks are often good picks for channel cats or small blues in medium-sized to large streams. Live crawfish make great bait in streams of all sizes and for cats of all kinds, although they won't account for many really big flatheads or blues.

Big pieces of cut bait work best for big blues, and live fish can't be beat for big flatheads. What fishermen need to figure out in any given river is what kinds of fish are mainstay food sources. Bream, for example, are favored baits for big flatheads in many coastal rivers and in reservoirs. On big rivers like the Mississippi, however, which don't offer much good habitat for bream, live gizzard shad work far better for catching flatheads. Similarly, when young-of-the-year anadromous shad abound in tidal rivers, blues really tend to key on them, and nothing makes better cut bait.

Anglers who prefer to use the current to their advantage fish primarily with dip baits, whether commercially manufactured or home-brewed. These type of baits, many of which have a cheese base, send an oily scent akin to a chum line downstream, and cats follow the scent right to the bait. The upper ends of river runs that have good current pushing though them are ideal places to set up with dip baits in streams of all sizes.

The trick is getting set up upstream of the most catfish but keeping the bait container downwind!

Lakes and Reservoirs

"There it is," George Logan announced, obviously pleased to have located the isolated rockpile he had been seeking. "And there are fish on it!" he added, his slight smile having given way to a wholesale grin.

Logan, a longtime flathead fisherman from Winston-Salem, North Carolina, has invested a lot of time targeting flatheads on a chain of reservoirs along the Yadkin River. Over time he has learned the kind of structure and cover that reservoir flatheads relate to through the seasons.

A century ago, most southern catfishermen didn't need to know much about still-water fishing. Except in Florida and through a narrow coastal plain strip along the Gulf and Atlantic coasts, the South doesn't have many natural lakes. And while natural lowland lakes do typically hold catfish, nearby rivers usually offer better catfishing.

The most noteworthy exceptions to the South's paucity of natural lakes come in the form of oxbows, historic bends in lowland rivers that have been fully or partially cut from main river channels to form lakes. Because of their riverine origins and association with the rivers they border, oxbows tend to offer very good catfishing, and the species makeup in any given one is generally the same as that in the river the lake was borne from.

Most oxbows, having formed from old riverbends, have the common denominator of being elongated and horseshoe shaped. Many oxbows remain connected to rivers at one end, at least during high-water conditions. Others are completely broken off. Most still have deep water on their outside bends and very good cover on shallow, inside-bend flats.

The best fishing varies dramatically from oxbow to oxbow and often from week to week, especially on those oxbows that remain connected to rivers. When rivers surge, cats will often move out of the main channel to the more protected waters of oxbows. Oxbows that are cut off from main rivers tend to offer the most stable fishing, and many get minimal fishing pressure because access is difficult. However, those that remain connected receive nutrients as well as baitfish and catfish from the river, and tend to produce more and larger catfish overall.

Natural lakes of all kinds make up only a tiny piece of today's still-water catfishing puzzle. Most waters named as "lakes" throughout the South are actually reservoirs, built for power generation, flood control or navigation. Rivers are full of energy in their natural state, and as America became more industrialized and populated through the 20th century, demand grew to harness some of that energy through the building of hydroelectric dams and consequently reservoirs. Hundreds of major reservoirs now dot southern landscapes, providing a lot of waters for anglers to explore.

Modern catfishermen would be mistaken to ignore the offerings of reservoirs. Beyond providing literally millions of acres of fishing waters, reservoirs tend to produce big catfish. Looking at line-class world records in *Fresh Water Angling Records* (2002), more than a dozen southern reservoirs are represented in the listings for flatheads, blues, and channels.

Nutrient levels are often higher in reservoirs than on the free-flowing portions of the rivers they impound. Therefore, they can support a hefty biomass of baitfish and predators, including big cats. Reservoirs also provide abundant habitat for plenty of fish and give catfish room to grow.

Finding the best catfishing on reservoirs, however, is often more difficult than finding the best fishing on rivers. Vast expanses in many reservoirs don't hold many fish, and sometimes the best structure lies buried beneath many feet of water. Anglers often need good lake maps and electronics and an understanding of how to use both to find the most or biggest fish.

Various reservoirs also vary dramatically in character and in the makeup of their catfish and baitfish populations. Some are shallow and warm and spread over vast areas. Others are narrow and channelized, looking little different than the unimpounded sections of the river they are built along. Despite many variances, most reservoirs do have certain common denominators in terms of the types of areas that catfish tend to favor.

The first thing that anglers should keep in mind when they think about reservoirs is that catfish are river fish, and they relate heavily to river channels and features along those channels even when those channels are buried under 30 feet of water. Flatheads, even more so than other kinds of cats, will almost always be in the vicinity of a major channel. Even if they are not down in the channel, they will be on a rockpile or brushpile that is beside a channel ledge or atop a hump that sets inside a bend in the river.

Flatheads will relate to main river channels from early fall through the first part of spring and will usually be close to submerged cover in a reservoir's open main body. During late spring and often though the summer, flatheads will move up tributary channels and will spawn in shoreline cavities. Even up the creeks, flatheads will generally favor cover along the channel side.

Adult blue catfish will roam open waters more freely than flatheads will, usually following schools of baitfish. However, they typically will only use a lake's main body and waters up major tributaries. Blues like big rivers, even within reservoirs, and they typically don't make much use of smaller creek arms. As a broad generalization, blues tend to congregate in the deep lower ends of lakes during the cooler months and move up river arms in the summer.

Channel catfish, like their cousins, relate to channel drops and use creek and river channels as travel routes up and down reservoirs. They use main rivers and creeks alike, however, and often will be

Figure 7. In reservoirs, adult blue catfish tend to relate to main-lake open areas or waters up major river arms. Mark Wiese of Toccoa, Georgia, pulled this blue from the Tennessee River channel in the upper portion of Watts Bar Lake.

found far from channel edges. Channel cats up to about 10 pounds can be found almost year 'round on many reservoirs around any shallow structure that has deep water close to it. Fishermen don't need a lot of specialized knowledge to locate creek mouths, prominent points, or sandbars that are apt to hold channel cats.

Whatever species they target, anglers who are unfamiliar with a reservoir cannot go wrong by beginning with a topographical map that shows where the main creek and river channels run. They can then either look for unique features along the channel, such as hard bends, deep holes or creek confluences, or look for other types of structure and cover in the vicinity of the channels.

Points and humps rank among the most consistently productive natural structural features on almost all reservoirs. Both provide fish a good variety of depths in a small area. The best points or humps, naturally, are those that stretch close to channel edges and that have some type of cover, such as stumps, brush, or rocks, atop them. Creek mouths are also great areas to concentrate fishing efforts, especially during the spring, when more cats move up tributaries and when frequent rains often supercharge creeks with assorted foodstuff.

Various man-made features also tend to hold a lot of catfish in reservoirs. Bridge crossings, dams, and riprap banks are among the best. Bridges, which often have channels cutting beneath them, provide abundant cover and structure. Many also have riprap causeways, which provide additional cover and tend to funnel baitfish, catfish, and current.

Dams, like bridges, offer expansive cover, and the deepest water in a reservoir is generally close to its dam. Underwater currents, created when water is poured though dams to generate electricity, also tend to concentrate cats and make them more active. Channel edges and tops of humps near dams can be outstanding when the water is moving.

The deep water around dams also provides thermal refuge for baitfish through midwinter on many southern reservoirs. Shad or herring ball up in the deep water, and catfish congregate beneath them. Anglers who brave the winter sometimes enjoy fast action using freshly netted baitfish.

At the opposite end of the calendar year, reservoir catfishermen must keep in mind that most southern reservoirs stratify during mid-summer, with the coolest, most oxygen-deficient water forming the bottom layer. While catfish don't require the same high levels of dissolved oxygen as some other species do, they often do require more than is in the bottom layer.

Because catfish are so closely associated with deep holes in rivers, reservoir fishermen sometimes make the mistake of fishing too deep in the summer. In lakes that stratify, the best spots often will be structural features with bottom depths that are within or above the thermocline, which is the moderate middle layer. That may include the tops or side of humps or points near the main channel, tributary channels that aren't as deep as the main river, or the river channel itself through the upper half of a lake.

Finally, as reservoir anglers study maps and consider holding areas, they should consider that most reservoirs do have some current pushing through portions of them, at times at least. Current strength varies from spot to spot within most reservoirs and from time to time, based on whether water is being run through upstream or downstream dams.

While reservoirs are essentially still-water destinations, catfishermen are still wise to carefully consider "current" conditions.

Ponds

Like those little glass Coke bottles that bring back fond memories to so many people, ponds and the catfish that often abound in them lie in the midst of many catfishermen's favorite fishing memories.

That's not to say that pond catfish are just for kids or other beginners. While pond fishing in its purest form is unapologetically basic, it's also great fun even to the most grizzled big-river catfishermen. There's something that is simply enjoyable about sitting in the shade of an old oak tree along the banks of a pond and waiting for the line to race off and the rod tip to bow.

In truth, a pond is nothing more than a small lake or reservoir, and there is no official number of acres or shoreline feet that delineates one from the other. Generally speaking, if somebody could see most of the shore from most places on a body of still water, he probably would call it a pond. From a fishing standpoint, most pond fishing is done either from the banks or from small johnboats, most of which stay pond-side throughout the year.

Through much of the South, most ponds are man-made. Impounded sections along creeks, which are typically backed up by simple earthen dams, most ponds are essentially miniature reservoirs. They have inundated creek arms beneath them, and their shape generally is formed by the lay of the land—just like reservoirs. Major differences are in the normal catfish population and forage makeup and the ways people typically fish.

One unique thing about ponds is that many are managed specifically for fishing. More specifically, many are managed for catfishing. "Pay per day" ponds, which abound throughout the South, are heavily stocked with channel catfish on a regular basis. Likewise, public fishing ponds operated by state fisheries agencies in several southern states are managed largely or exclusively as catfishing ponds.

Most ponds in the South have bullheads and/or channel catfish in them. Where bullheads are the only cats in a pond, they may get some targeted fishing pressure. Where channels also exist, bullheads typically are only caught as a by-catch. Some state-managed fishing ponds also get stocked with some blue catfish. Many pay-per-day ponds also have a handful of trophy blues and flatheads in them, which are stocked as "wild cards" for fishermen and can only be taken from the pond if an angler is willing to pay a hefty "trophy fee."

Neither channels nor blues tend to even approach their full size potential in ponds, which may be largely based on the normal forage available. Both species turn heavily to diets of shad as they gain size in natural river systems, and many ponds don't have any shad in them. Pond catfish generally subsist on aquatic insects, assorted other invertebrates, minnows, and occasionally small sunfish.

While big catfish are not common in ponds, big numbers are the norm. Ponds not managed for fishing, whether in subdivisions or cow pastures, tend to get very light catfishing pressure, if they get fished at all. Often a good population of feisty channel cats or bullheads awaits whoever gains access to a pond and goes after them. Often, getting permission to fish is only a matter of asking.

Figure 8. Ponds are ideal places for family outings. The author's daughter, Sarah, caught this channel catfish from a Public Fishing Area pond in middle Georgia.

Owners of pay-per-day ponds, meanwhile, build their businesses on successful fishing trips. Therefore, they generally keep these waters very heavily stocked. Similarly, most ponds managed by fisheries agencies as fishing ponds are quite heavily stocked. The goal, with most of these ponds, is that families can go and sit on the banks and catch fish with neither a lot of specialized tackle nor extensive know-how.

Simplicity is the essence of pond fishing. Anglers pick a spot along the bank to fish from, bait up a couple of rods, cast them out, and wait for a rod tip to jiggle or bend down. Night crawlers, chicken livers, or hot dogs are tough to beat as bait, and the best rig, more often than not, involves nothing more than a hook and just enough weight to cast the offering and get it to the bottom.

The best hooks depend on the bait. For chicken livers, a No. 4 or No. 6 treble hook works great. For hot dogs and night crawlers, a long-shank single hook of roughly the same size works better. Generally speaking, a big split shot or small rubber-core sinker adds plenty of weight for casting and getting baits down in ponds.

Rods and reels used for pond fishing need not be any fancier than the terminal tackle. Any style of outfit—whether spinning, spin-casting, or baitcasting—that casts 10- or 12-pound-test easily will work for most pond-catfishing applications. A reel should have a drag that functions properly, just in case an angler does hook into a hefty cat. While big cats aren't the norm in most ponds, a few cats commonly escape being caught for several years and grow to large sizes.

As simple as pond fishing is, catching fish is not strictly a roll of the dice. Anglers who understand catfish behavior and apply that understanding to their fishing plan catch far more fish on a regular basis than anglers who approach the fishing randomly. Picking spots logically, experimenting with baits, and knowing when to move are all part of the equation.

For starters, some areas hold good concentrations of catfish almost all the time. A pond's dam and its creek channels, for example, are almost always good areas, and the single best area on many ponds is right around the old channel, near where it is dammed up.

Even from the bank, without the benefit of any electronics, anglers often can figure out where the channel runs in the vicinity of the dam by simply looking at where the creek comes out on the back side of the dam. At the opposite end of a pond, the orientation of the main creek as it opens up into the pond often provides a good clue as to which way the channel continues through the pond.

Whether near the dam or at the head of a pond, some catfish will almost always relate to the main channel. However, they won't necessarily be in the channel. Often, they will be on adjacent cover or structure, especially in the summer, when dissolved oxygen levels tend to be low in the deepest parts of many ponds.

Veteran anglers look at the lay of the land and try to figure out how the channel runs. Then they consider the best-looking spots that are adjacent to that channel. If the channel is within casting distance of the bank, across good structure, they can then put a bait in the channel and another atop adjacent structure to see which depth the cats are using.

Because ponds are small and often simple in form, likely fish-holding structure is generally easy to recognize. Any cove, for example, tends to reveal where a tributary runs. By sitting on the point, where a cove opens into a pond, an angler often can cast baits close to a significant channel confluence. Little points that stretch out from the banks, meanwhile, often go way out into ponds, under the water.

In ponds that are basically round or rectangular, which are not unusual because many pond sites get cleared and dug out prior to impoundment, any little change in the pitch of the bank often signals a depth break out in the pond that the fish will stack up along.

Along with bottom features, pond fishermen should also pay close attention to cover that stretches out from the banks. Bank fishermen always seem to want to cast as far out as they can, and by doing so in ponds they sometimes cast right past the cats. Catfish quite commonly will pile up around cover like riprap, a dam's spillway, or laydowns.

If cats don't cooperate in a spot, pond fishermen are generally better off moving than waiting for the fish to come their way. Subtle factors that would be difficult to pinpoint at the beginning of a day make some spots far better than others on any given day, and fishermen only find those spots by moving periodically.

In the same way, while chicken livers, hot dogs, or night crawlers will almost always produce some catfish if the fish are nearby, the cats in any given pond will favor one bait over another on many days. Whatever the reason, it's worthwhile for pond fishermen to carry a few different types of bait and test them all to see if the catfish have a preference.

In ponds that are really packed with catfish, neither the specific spot nor the bait makes a huge difference. In such cases, the spot with the broadest shade tree, the shortest walk from the car, or the flattest grassy bank for laying a blanket on is the best place to fish.

Similarly, if hopping from spot to spot isn't fun for the kids on a family outing, catching fewer fish is a small cost compared to keeping everyone happy. That factor is worth emphasizing because ponds, more so than any other types of waterways, lend themselves to family catfishing trips. Easy access and abundant, cooperative fish make for low-effort, high-reward trips, and those are the types of trips that nurture a fishing interest in kids and other newcomers to the sport.

Chapter 3

Chapter 3

Bait and Tackle

Natural Offerings

"That would be a good place to fish for catfish," my brother-in-law, Jerry Perry, mentioned casually, pointing to a treetop that stretched into the deepest part of a big hole. We had been fishing for smallmouths—officially, at least—but we were really fishing for all that would bite.

We had caught smallmouths, spots, largemouths, bluegills, and various other sunfish, but mention of catfish caught my attention. I looked to him for more instructions.

"Add a little weight about a foot up your line, cast just upstream of the tree and let the bait fall right down in the branches."

A fat cat must have read our script because my bait—a big hellgrammite that we had caught from the same creek—barely hit bottom before the line raced sideways. I set the hook with a snap, and my light spinning rod bent hard. A few minutes later, I was grinning foolishly as I admired a fat channel cat. Five minutes after that, I was admiring a cat that could have been the first one's twin.

Of all the things an angler can put on a hook in hopes of getting catfish to grab it, it is often tough to top those menu items that the fish normally feed on in a given waterway. Live fish and various critters that live in and around streams and lakes look, act, smell, and taste like real food to catfish because they *are* real food to catfish.

It would be tough to chronicle every living creature that could be used to catch catfish in the Southeastern United States. Here are some of the best, though, with a few words on where to get them, how to fish them, and what kinds of cats are most likely to eat them.

Worms

The classic fish bait for practically everything that swims in fresh water, worms work great for catching catfish. Any earthworm, of which many varieties exist, will produce catfish. However, big worms, especially night crawlers, will produce the fastest action overall. Worms attract strikes from all kinds of cats on occasion, but they won't connect anglers with many adult blue or flathead catfish.

Catfishermen can buy worms from almost any bait store, dig them up, or even farm them at home. The best spots to dig for worms are fertile, shaded areas that stay a bit moist. Also, any spot in the ground that produces worms once is apt to yield more the next time as well.

Catfish eat worms because they smell good, not because they look good, so most fisherman string the worm on the hook from one end to the other or hook it numerous times to "wad" it on.

Hellgrammites

The larvae of dobsonflies, hellgrammites like cool rocky streams and are nearly certain cat-catchers in any stream that supports them. Anglers who drift hellgrammites shouldn't plan on catching only catfish, though. Virtually everything that swims in a creek will eat a live hellgrammite, and the only real way to favor catfish is to get the baits in catfish holding areas.

An easy way to catch hellgrammites is to stretch a seine net crosscurrent and flip big rocks upstream of it. Lacking a seine or a good place to use one, flipping rocks in shallow water along the edge of a stream and catching the little critters by hand also works.

During midsummer, they'll sometimes burrow under shoreline rocks, just up from the normal water level.

Hellgrammites can pinch, so they should be handled carefully. Most anglers hook them through the head or underneath the collar and fish them with just enough weight added to the line to get them to the bottom in prime catfish lies.

Crawfish

Crawfish, which come in many varieties and live in and around lakes, rivers, and streams throughout the South, also serve as meals for many kinds of fish. Again, the key to catching cats on craws is to put the baits where catfish swim.

Large, live crawfish will produce some flatheads, especially in small to medium-sized rivers. Overall, however, crawfish work better for channel and white catfish, either of which will take them dead or alive. Some fishermen contend that they catch more fish on live crawfish when they twist the pincers off. Whether that's true or not, no one catches fewer catfish by doing so, and it probably saves some fishermen from being pinched! Most fishermen hook crawfish through the tail, in through the bottom and out the top.

Scattered bait stores sell crawfish. Usually, though, fishermen have to catch their own. In streams, mainstay tactics are flipping rocks or running seines. Various forms of traps, which can be baited with chicken parts, will also catch crawfish in still water or moving water.

Clams and Mussels

Vastly overlooked by catfishermen, various freshwater clams and mussels make up a big part of the food supply for cats in many waterways. Channel catfish and small to mid-sized blues, especially, feed extensively on Asiatic clams and various other mollusks.

Clams and mussels typically don't show up in the bait shop refrigerator, so anglers have to dig up their own. Along sandy banks, flats, or shallow points, most anglers either feel for them with bare feet or use a small shovel and sifter to search them out. A mollusk will work as bait right out of its shell, which can be pried open or cracked with a screwdriver or hammer. However, some catfishermen prefer to leave clams and mussels out in the sun to "ripen" for a couple of days.

Shad

Shad of all sizes make up an important part of the catfishing equation, and fishermen use shad in many different forms. Small strips of cut bait produce fast action where channels or white cats abound. At the same time, gizzard shad weighing more than a pound are commonly put down as live bait for heavyweight flatheads. Meanwhile, whole dead threadfin shad or large chunks of cut gizzard shad account for a lot of trophy blues.

Fresh shad can be spread out on traditional bottom rigs, dragged with drift-fishing rigs or bounced in heavy current with three-way rigs, to name just a few options. Depending on the size of the shad and the size of cats sought, anglers may use one or more whole shad or cut the baitfish into slices.

Big live shad make great flathead bait in tailwaters or other areas where flatheads see far more shad than bream. They also make good picks in states where bream cannot be used legally as bait.

Bait dealers sell shad in many locations, especially around lakes and rivers that are known for good striper fishing. Anglers who prefer to gather their own baitfish can locate them either by watching for them flipping on the surface or by seeking schools out with a graph or flasher. Most fishermen then use castnets to catch the shad. Small-mesh dipnets also work in some instances, especially against dams or other structural features that can be used to help corral the shad.

Caught or bought, shad should be fresh, most catfishermen contend. Shad that have been frozen lose a lot of their appeal, and they don't stay on a hook very well.

Herring

Many veteran fishermen contend that a big chunk of fresh herring is the best bait that can be put out for really big blue catfish. Very oily fish, skipjack and blueback herring put out a lot of scent in the water. Plus, they are important natural forage to big blues in many waterways.

Like shad, herring can be used alive or dead, and baitfish of all sizes are useful. Popular applications are similar for shad and herring, except that many veteran anglers will use herring first, given a

Figure 9. Often it's tough to beat the foods that catfish are accustomed to eating. Many anglers consider cut skipjack herring the bait of choice for heavyweight blue catfish in waters that support a lot of skipjack.

choice of either, for cut bait. Fishermen cut big herring a lot of different ways, but the most popular technique is to "steak" them, making cuts across the body that are an inch or so thick.

Herring are predators, feeding on small shad and other tiny baitfish, so they often can be caught more easily on a rod and reel than with a net. Jigs or spoons work great for big skipjack or blueback herring, which feed best in current. Smaller herring, which hold in big schools, can be netted or cast for with Sabiki Rigs, which are strings of tiny jigs or flashy flies.

Bream

Where legal, live sunfish of various species, collectively known as "bream" throughout the South, are easily the most popular flathead baits. Where there is water, there are bream in this part of the country, which makes them a great live-bait choice for a couple of reasons. First, they are typically available. Second, flatheads are used to seeing them and eating them in most lakes and rivers. Bream also survive better in a live well than many other species of forage fish do.

Most catfishermen hook bream through the back, near the end of the spiny dorsal fin, being careful not to pierce the spine, and then hang them just off the bottom. At night, many anglers let big bream run where they will on free-lines, and those bream sometimes find their way into the mouths of huge, hungry flatheads.

Other Naturals

The list of "other" live-bait options could go on for a long time, but some of the other baits that catfishermen most commonly turn to include grasshoppers, catalpa worms, wasp larvae, eels (whole and cut), minnows, smaller catfish, frogs, carp, suckers, and various small gamefish, where legal.

The mention of legality warrants highlighting. Each state has its own set of laws regarding what can and cannot be used as bait and how bait can and cannot be captured. Various gamefish and exotic species cannot be used as bait in some states. It's vital that anglers check state laws before keeping anything or using it as bait.

Not-So-Natural Offerings

The list of things no one has ever caught a catfish on might be shorter than the list of things that have been used with success by innovative catfish anglers. Channel cats, white cats, and bullheads have rarely been accused of being finicky feeders. If something smells interesting, they are apt to give it a try. For that reason, a lot of things that aren't natural foods for cats still work very well as catfish bait.

Looking at not-so-natural offerings, it is probably best to begin by defining the term. Some very popular catfish baits, like chicken livers and hot dogs, are natural in the strictest sense. They come from animals, not laboratories. They are not, however, foods that catfish find and eat in their natural environment.

Frozen shrimp sort of fall between natural and unnatural because shrimp do coexist with catfish in brackish water, and there are freshwater species of shrimp. That said, most shrimp used as catfish bait are of the saltwater variety, and most popular catfishing waters are indeed fresh.

As was the case with the natural offerings, this coverage is far from exhaustive. Such a look could be a book in itself. The idea is to highlight some of the bait types that southern catfishermen most commonly catch the most catfish on, and to look at how and when to fish each.

Manufactured Baits

Commercially manufactured catfish baits come in forms that range from little dog food–like chunks to tubs of mushy goo. The common denominator of virtually all manufactured baits is that they smell dreadful. Man's dread can be a catfish's delight, however, and fish can smell these baits from a long ways away.

Quality catfish baits don't simply stink, however. They have purposeful stinkiness. While any sour-smelling doughy mix may catch bullheads, the best catfish baits are mixed using cheese or some type of high-tech high-amino-acid base that smells like something meaty. Meaty scents and flavors, like shad and blood, attract bigger cats overall, because as catfish grow larger, they tend to turn more to high-protein menu items.

Dip baits probably top the popularity charts among manufactured catfish baits. Gooey concoctions that typically come in tubs,
they are designed to be used either with sponges or special worms,
which, as the bait name suggests, anglers dip in the bait.

Most dip bait manufacturers also produce "catfish" worms.
The worms can take a couple of basic forms, and they often come
rigged, each with a leader and treble hook. Some are strips of rubber tubing with holes punched in them. Others are short, thickly
ribbed worms. Either way (or with a more traditional sponge), the
idea is to have something that holds the bait in place but still allows
some bait to break up and escape. That way the scent spreads and
makes a trail to the bait for the fish to follow.

Figure 10. A lot of catfishermen really like dip baits, especially for channel
catfish. The best dips have a strong "meaty" smell and are tough
enough to stay on a hook, but soft enough to break up some in a
current.

With dip baits, consistency sets side-by-side with scent and flavor, in terms of importance. A bait must be sufficiently thick and sticky to stay intact for a while, even in current, but thin enough to break up gradually. Of course, different conditions call for different consistencies, so fishermen really have to experiment to find the dips that work best for them under a variety of conditions and in different places.

One accessory that is all but essential for fishing with most dip baits is a stick to mash the worm or sponge down into the dip. Dip baits are best kept in the tubs they come in or on the end of the line—and nowhere else.

Catfish nuggets rely on the same "meaty" types of scents and flavors as dips do, with flavors like cheese, shad, blood, and liver. The difference, from a rigging standpoint, is that the nuggets go directly on a hook. Nugget-type baits don't send out as much scent as dips do, but they are far easier and less messy to use, and they stay on the hook better.

If cats are concentrated and either style of bait will do the job, there's no reason to mess with dip. Or, if strong currents or very hot weather (which thins dips) makes it too hard to keep worms baited, nuggets become better choices. Fishermen who run trotlines or limblines also like to use nuggets because the bait typically stays on the hook until a fish grabs it.

It's worth noting, also, that manufactured does not necessarily mean commercially manufactured. Home-brewed "stinkbaits" were popular long before fishing companies began creating and selling catfish bait, and many anglers still prefer their own concoctions. Every recipe and mixing process is unique, and many are well-guarded secrets. However, most include some type of strong cheese and involve some aging.

Chicken Livers

Arguably, nothing is more widely known for its cat-attracting capabilities than a chicken liver. Of course, anyone who has fished with livers knows the reason for their popularity. Meaty, juicy, and stinky, chicken livers quite simply make outstanding catfish bait.

Livers work in rivers and lakes, both big and small, and under all kinds of conditions. They'll yield very few really big blues and

even fewer large flatheads, but they work wonderfully well for channels, bullheads, whites, and even small blues. They're also cheap
and available at any grocery store.

The biggest downfall of chicken livers is that they can be a bit
touchy to keep on the hook at first. Once livers have been in the
water a while, they get pretty tough. Initially, however, they're apt
to fly off on the cast. A couple of things help quite a bit in that
regard. The first is rig up with a treble hook and wrap about half a
liver onto the hook, jabbing it several times. The second is to lob
the rig, instead of making a quick cast.

Chicken livers are also dreadfully messy to fish with. A hand
towel is as important for fishing with livers as a stick is for fishing
with dip bait.

Shrimp

Shrimp offer the same basic appeal as crawfish. The difference is
that they are more readily available than their crustacean cousins
in grocery stores and some bait shops. They make great bait for
channel cats of all sizes and for white catfish. Depending on the size
of the shrimp and the size of the catfish, shrimp can be fished whole
or broken into pieces.

Shrimp make pretty expensive bait except in areas where bait
shops carry shrimp that have been packaged and frozen specifically
for bait use. Most, but not all, bait shops that stock frozen shrimp in
their freezers are located near the coast. Some inland shops that are
close to popular catfishing rivers and lakes do stock shrimp for the
purpose of catfishing.

Of course, since shrimp come frozen, anglers who don't live
near the coast can always stock up on catfish bait when they take
vacations at the beach.

Blood

While not widely used in the South, blood is one of the most popular baits used by serious catfishermen through much of the Midwest.
Virtually all the anglers that fish a couple of major catfish tournament circuits in the Upper Midwest fish exclusively with blood,
and "blood fishermen" from Nebraska have won the National

Championship Catfish Tournament, held annually on South Carolina's Santee Cooper Lakes, a couple of times.

The blood that these guys fish with isn't any kind of blood-flavored bait. It's blood, literal cow blood, gotten fresh from local slaughterhouses. They cool it for several days, which causes it to coagulate to a gelatin consistency, and then cut it into cubes. The blood is as messy to fish with as one would expect, and hooking it so it will stay on the hook is a science in itself. Like liver, though, blood toughens after it's been in the water for a while.

Most anglers drift with blood, bouncing it on or near the bottom. They seek out cats, instead of waiting for the cats to find them, and leave a trail as they go. The blood constantly dissolves, so it's sort of like chum and bait combined.

Blood works very well on blue and channel catfish of all sizes. However, most fishermen who drift blood don't catch many really small fish, simply because they generally use large pieces of bait. Blood produces only occasional flatheads.

Fridge Baits

Anglers headed to local ponds never have to leave home to collect their bait. In fact, they can gather bait and make lunch at the same time, because many of the best baits for bullheads and farm pond channel catfish are found in just about every home refrigerator in the country.

Hot dogs probably head the list of fine refrigerator baits for cats. A small strip of hot dog typically won't stay on the bottom long if there are catfish nearby. Cheap hot dogs work as well as expensive ones, but chicken and turkey dogs tend to not stay on the hook as well as those made of beef or pork. Small treble hooks work well for keeping dogs on the hook and for hooking catfish.

Bacon offers similar appeal and brings a little extra toughness. It's generally more expensive than hot dogs, though, and won't necessarily produce more fish for the money.

Cheese also works very well for channel cats and especially for bullheads. Consistency is probably more important than flavor in picking varieties of cheeses, with the best ones being soft and slow to crumble.

For ponds that have mostly bullheads in them, bread is the simplest and least expensive option. A nice wad of sticky white bread, wrapped around a small treble hook, works great for bullheads. However, all but the smallest channels will more readily take a meat or cheese offering than they will a wad of bread.

Rods and Reels

Pan-sized farm-pond channel catfish and 50-pound big-river blues obviously call for very different kinds of gear. The only common denominator among all catfish tackle is that it needs to be made to last.

Casting heavy weights, handling sticky bait, propping rods up along dirt banks, and fighting powerful fish in strong currents all have the potential to break down tackle. Whether big or small, rods and reels must able to handle a bit of grit and grime, and extra wear and tear, if they are to cut it as catfish gear.

For cats that weigh less than about 10 pounds, durability is really the only significant criterion. Spinning, spincasting, and baitcasting outfits will all work in most situations, according to an angler's preferences, and there's no single rod length or action that's necessarily best suited for the task.

For ponds or creeks, lightweight outfits work best. With light rods and reels, anglers can spool up with 8- or 10-pound test and cast split-shot rigs or other lightly weighted offerings decent distances. Plus, light rods and reels make even small catfish a barrel of fun to catch.

For many lake- and river-fishing applications, most fishermen prefer medium-action spinning or baitcasting outfits, like bass anglers typically use. Even if the cats aren't any bigger, rigs weighted with an ounce or more of weight call for a little heavier gear. Some anglers also like spincasting gear, which the line almost never gets twisted in. Solidly made spincasting reels on fiberglass rods make very good channel cat outfits, and they are great for kids because of their simplicity of operation.

Bigger cats obviously demand bigger gear. Likewise, strong currents and big water often dictate anglers up-sizing their gear.

Whether cats weigh 3 pounds or 30 pounds, it takes a fairly stout rod to handle casting several ounces of weight or bouncing a couple ounces of lead and a big chunk of bait along the bottom in a strong tailwater current.

Some anglers like flippin' sticks matched with baitcasting reels for a broad range of catfishing applications. These heavy-action bass rods can handle a fair amount of weight and have enough backbone to handle decent-sized cats. They are also typically 7 to 7½ feet long, which allows anglers to make fairly long casts.

Tailwater catfishermen, especially those who cast from the banks, sometimes need to make extremely long casts. They gear up with surf-casting rods that are often more than 10 feet long and match them up with big spinning or baitcasting reels that hold a lot of line. These fishermen prefer tough fiberglass rods that they can cast several ounces of weight with and bang on the rocks on occasion.

Catfishermen who rig up with big chunks of cut shad or live bream don't mess around with gear that might not do the job on a heavyweight cat. Fish that commonly exceed 50 pounds pull like few other freshwater fish, and pushy big-river currents sometimes make big cats extra tough to muscle in.

In waters inhabited by big blues and flatheads, most serious catfish anglers like rods that are 7 to 8 feet long, with a medium-heavy or heavy action, plenty of backbone, and enough beef to comfortably cast several ounces of weight. Most catfish anglers prefer fiberglass or E-Glass rods over graphite rods for their toughness and lifting power. Night fishermen prefer white rods, especially those that have fluorescent tips, because they are much easier to see at night than dark rods.

As for reels, most serious catfishermen who target really big cats like baitcasting gear because baitcasters offer more winching power. They like geared-down baitcasting reels that hold a lot of line, have smooth drag systems, and are equipped with clickers to signal bites. Some anglers do prefer spinning reels, especially with extra-long rods used for tailwater fishing.

A handful of rod-and-reel manufactures make rods, reels, and rod/reel combinations specifically with catfishermen in mind. They cover a fairly broad range of sizes and fishing applications.

Figure II. Different catfishing situations call for different types of gear. For big cats, though, many anglers like fairly heavy E-Glass rods matched with conventional reels.

Hook, Line, and Sinker

The vital link between fish and fishermen, an angler's line ranks right up there in importance with the bait laid out and the rod and reel in-hand. If the line breaks, the game ends. Also essential are an angler's hooks, weights, and other terminal gear. If those aren't right, the fish never gets hooked in the first place.

Line

Because catfish live on the bottom, often among rubble and tree-tops or over mussel beds, and because cats have sandpaper-like teeth, abrasion resistance is the most important characteristic of any catfish line. Whether it's 10-pound-test monofilament or 100-pound-test braid, line must be able to take a beating.

Line size correlates primarily with fish size, so since catfish come in an awfully big range of sizes, preferred line weights also vary quite a bit. For all classes of cats, anglers do better to err heavy than light. Catfish feed primarily by smell, not by sight, so line shyness rarely presents a problem.

For farm-pond bullhead and channels, 8- or 10-pound test will do the job. In larger rivers and lakes, anglers need more weight to keep their baits in place, and a little bigger fish sometimes show up. Therefore, most fishermen go with 14-, 17-, or 20-pound test. For heavyweight flatheads and blues or big-water conditions, serious catfishermen rarely spool up with anything lighter than 30-pound test. Anglers commonly use 40- and 50-pound-test for big cats, and some go notably heavier.

Most major line manufacturers make several varieties of line, each with unique qualities, which leaves anglers with a lot of questions to sort through. Catfishermen seek line that rates high in abrasion resistance and shock strength. Night fishermen also prefer highly visible, even fluorescent, line.

Many catfishermen also really like copolymers, which are tough and strong but are also easy to cast and tie. For leaders, some catfishermen prefer fluorocarbon leader material, which is exceedingly abrasion resistant but quite stiff and somewhat expensive.

Also popular among big-cat specialists are braided and fused lines, made of braided or heat-fused high-tech microfibers. These offer much greater strength in smaller diameters than traditional lines, and very little stretch.

Big-river fishermen like these lines because they can use very heavy tests and still keep a small diameter that won't get dragged as much by strong currents. Many drifters and other anglers who stretch out very long lines like "super lines," as they are sometimes called, for their low-stretch qualities, which help the anglers detect strikes and get solid hooksets.

Hooks

If line choices are overwhelming, hook choices are mind-boggling. Many hook styles have very specific applications, however, most of which little to do with catfishing. A handful of basic hook styles will meet most catfishing needs, as long as hooks are matched to bait sizes.

In terms of sizes, catfishermen commonly use everything from No. 4 hooks for fishing live hellgrammites to 10/O hooks for fishing big chunks of cut skipjack. Hooks in the 2/O to 4/O range probably get the most overall use among catfishermen. Big-cat specialists mostly use 5/O and larger hooks.

Some of the most popular hook styles for a broad range of catfishing applications include O'Shaughnessy, wide-gap, baitholder, treble, and circle hooks. Several manufacturers make some version of each, and most catfishermen have specific favorites based on various factors, among them sharpness, cost, toughness, and design variances.

O'Shaughnessy hooks, which are heavy-wire steel hooks that are also popular with bait fishermen in saltwater settings, have a very basic design that gives them great all-around catfishing appeal. Tru-Turn Catfish Hooks use an O'Shaughnessy design.

Wide-gap designs, which include Kahle hooks, are popular among fishermen who use big chunks of cut bait or other thick baits.

Baitholder hooks, meanwhile, are most popular in smaller sizes. Baitholders have small barbs on the shank to keep night crawlers or other natural offerings from slipping down them.

Treble hooks are best for keeping soft bait, like chicken livers, on the hook. Small trebles also are almost certain to hook channels or bullheads. However, anglers must set the hooks quickly with trebles, because they are tough to get out of deeply hooked catfish.

Figure 12. Serious catfishermen stay well stocked with a good assortment of heavy-duty terminal tackle, especially hooks, weights, and swivels.

As important as it is for anglers using treble hooks to set the hook quickly, anglers who tie on circle hooks must train them-selves to *not* set the hook. The fish hook themselves, usually in the corner of the mouth, as they swim away, and a hookset often will pull the hook from the fish's mouth. Circle hooks are becoming increasingly popular with catfishermen because they do hook fish in the mouth most of the time, which makes it much easier to release fish in good condition.

Weights

Since catfish spend most of their time on or near the bottom, often in deep water and beneath strong currents, most catfish rigs include weights. Like hooks, weights come in all different shapes, but again a handful of basic designs get the lion's share of use by catfishermen.

Starting with the smallest and simplest weights that catfisher-men ever add to their lines, split shot work great when catfish are shallow and fishermen want realistic presentations for natural baits. Anglers fishing with night crawlers, crawfish, or hellgrammites in small streams, for example, generally want their baits to tumble in the current and fall slowly into holes, where catfish await with open mouths. Some fishermen also use split shot to peg sliding weights.

Anglers who want just a little more weight than a shot offers but who want to keep their rigs simple sometimes turn to rubber-core weights. The line is tucked into a slit in the side of the weight and then wrapped around an inserted rubber core. Easy to put on and take off or move up and down lines, rubber core weights work perfectly when anglers need just a little bit of weight for fishing ponds or lake coves.

Egg weights, which, as the name suggests, are shaped like eggs, are easily the most broadly used style of weight by catfishermen. They are readily available in sizes that range from an eighth of an ounce to several ounces. The line simply goes through a hole that runs lengthwise through the weight. Most egg weights are either pegged with a split shot or slid on the main line, above a swivel.

Bell sinkers, which are bell shaped and have a metal eye molded on top of them, are sometimes substituted for egg weights on sliding rigs because they won't roll down slopes or down the river as readily. More commonly, they are used to peg three-way rigs. Also popular for three-ways rigs are bank sinkers, which are similar to bell sinkers but more elongated, molded entirely of lead, and often available in larger sizes.

Anglers who drift and drag rigs across the bottom use various styles of sinkers, all designed to bounce along the bottom without getting caught in every brushpile or gap between rocks.

Swivels

Swivels, which are part of most catfish rigs, serve a few important purposes. First, they link components. Second, they serve as stoppers for sliding weights. Third, and most importantly, they keep main lines from getting twisted when baits spin in the current.

Catfishermen commonly use two main styles of swivels: barrel swivels and three-way swivels. Barrel swivels, which have a rotating barrel in the middle and eyes at each end, divide main line and leader in basic sliding-sinker rigs. Three-way swivels, which have three eyes situated in triangular fashion, form the center of three-way rigs. Whatever the style, catfishermen should use only heavy-duty, high-quality swivels that are rated for at least as many pounds of pressure as the test rating of their line.

Floats

Since cats stay deep, more often than not, many fishermen don't associate floats with catfishing. In truth, though, floats actually serve a few important catfishing functions.

First, floats can be used to suspend baits just off the bottom or next to cover. Around thick cover and strong currents, especially, dangling a bait under a float may be the only way to get the offering close to the catfish's lair. A slip cork, which slides freely on the line, works best if the fish are more than about four feet deep. A bobber stop, which will slide through rod eyes but not the end of the slip cork, is used to set the depth that the float will suspend the bait.

Flathead fishermen commonly add huge slip corks for river fishing. With a cork that's big enough to support several ounces of lead, they can dangle a big live bait just off the bottom and right next to cover that they cannot get the boat beside. Flathead fishermen's slip corks are commonly five or six inches long.

Beyond suspending baits, corks are sometimes used by drift-fishermen to keep hooks up off the bottom. A drifter will actually put a small float between his weight and his hook. The weight still drags bottom, but the hook stays a couple feet up from the bottom, saving a lot of snags.

Finally, floats can serve as strike indicators. With inexperienced anglers, especially, it often helps to have a very visual indicator of what's happening under the surface. Even if cats are on the bottom and a float is set a little deeper than the bottom depth, kids and other newcomers to the sport learn quickly to set the hook when the float takes off in a hurry.

Putting Things Together

Catfishermen link their terminal tackle in dozens of ways to fit specific circumstances. However, most commonly used rigs are some variation of either a Carolina rig or a three-way rig.

The Carolina rig, also called a sliding-sinker rig, uses a weight, a barrel swivel, and a hook. The main line runs through the weight, which is usually an egg weight, and is tied to one end of the swivel. Some anglers add a bead to protect the knot. A piece of leader, which can be the same material as the main line or something different, is then tied to the other end of the swivel and a hook is tied to the end of it.

The three-way rig centers on a three-way swivel, to which the main line is tied to one eye and a section of leader to each of the others. A hook goes at the end of one leader (usually the longer piece). A weight, usually a bell or bank sinker, goes on the end of the other leader. In snag-filled waters, anglers use lighter leader material for their weight than for their hook or main line. That way, if the weight gets unsalveagably snagged, a piece of lead is all that gets lost.

Electronics

When the first crude fish finders were introduced many years ago, fishermen everywhere cried out that such modernization would mark the beginning of the end for sport fishing. Surely, the ability to locate fish would make fishing too easy and soon there wouldn't be any fish left to catch.

It didn't take long for folks to figure out that knowing fish were in a spot and getting those fish to bite didn't necessarily go hand-in-hand. They also learned pretty quickly that the new fish finders didn't tell anglers whether the fish they were looking at were bass, buffalo, catfish, or carp.

As sport catfishing has grown more serious and catfishermen have become more sophisticated, electronic devices have become a much bigger part of the catfishing equation. Anglers rely on graphs, flashers, and various other electronic devices to find spots and figure out how and where to set up.

While they still call their sonar units "fish finders," veteran catfishermen use their graphs and flashers for much more than finding fish. They use flashers to quickly recognize channel breaks and locate scattered schools of baitfish and graphs to study bottom contours, search out clusters of cover, examine groups of catfish and baitfish, and identify thermal layers, among other things.

Since the mid-1990s, when Global Positioning System (GPS) technology reached the popular fishing market, many catfishermen have bought either GPS units to complement their other electronics or graphs with GPS built into them. Using satellite readings, GPS units track where fishermen are. The fishermen can save specific "waypoints" and return to those spots simply by following the leading of the GPS unit. Many catfishermen have GPS units with lake maps programmed into them, and they have saved waypoints for their favorite spots.

Many anglers like to use flashers and graphs together, because flashers operate faster than graphs and give immediately accurate depth readings both for the bottom and for things between the boat and the bottom. Anglers who are attuned to their flashers can watch the little round screens as they ride and quickly recognize changes in the bottom contour or schools of baitfish.

Other nifty electronic gadgets that some anglers rely on are special temperature and dissolved oxygen monitors, which use probes on lines to measure temps and oxygen levels at specific depths. Both readings can be valuable in midsummer, when cats, like other fish, seek thermal refuge but dissolved oxygen levels sometimes run low in deep water.

Graphs, the electronic units that catfishermen rely most heavily upon, vary enormously in capacities and picture quality—and in price. River fishermen who only want to know where holes begin sloping off so they know where to anchor need nothing fancier than the most basic graph on the market. Other anglers use virtually every feature on even the most sophisticated units.

Drift-fishermen, for example, watch their graphs constantly. They pay close attention to fish sizes, positions and depths, baitfish abundance, bottom contours and makeup, water temperatures, and much more, and they often track their drifts with GPS so they can repeat the ones that produce fish. Because drifters cover a lot of water, with a range of conditions, they want to know as much as they can about any spot that yields strikes.

Drift-fishermen and still fishermen alike use GPS units and their built-in maps to guide them directly to favorite offshore humps, ditches, and creek-channel confluences. They ride straight to spots they previously could find only through careful triangulation and hard searching with graphs.

Most fishermen who use their graphs quite a bit to find fish prefer units that offer true readings over those that make fish symbols. They prefer to interpret what they see on their own and use experience to learn differences in the appearance of marks made by various sizes and kinds of fish.

Factors anglers might consider in picking a graph, beyond price, include the number of pixels, which dictate resolution, the specific features individual units offer, and the way screens are set up. If the opportunity exists and an angler isn't in a huge hurry to get a graph, the best way to compare units, by far, is to pay attention to and even play with graphs in a few friends' boats and see how they perform on the water. Explanations of specs and features are overwhelming in catalogs and stores and of only modest value unless linked with some practical experience.

On the water, the best way to learn to read a specific graph is simply to invest a lot of time staring at it. Anglers who have owned a few graphs know the value of getting to know their units. They typically will take new graphs to very familiar ledges or brushpiles just to see how those features show up on the screen. Similarly, when the catfish are really biting, as tough as it may be to stop fishing for a while, there's no better time to pull anchor and ride back and forth over the fish to see exactly what they look like on the graph.

Generally speaking, catfish are usually on or quite near the bottom. Flatheads generally stay close to main channels and tight to some type of cover. They are usually either alone or in small groups. Many anglers contend that flatheads that are barely off the bottom, instead of laying flat on it, are most likely to bite. They also remain more confident that flatheads will bite if fish they set up over move around on occasion.

Channel cats will usually be in fairly big groups. They will be scattered all over the bottom of areas they are using but will be concentrated near the main breaks along the edges of those features.

Slopes at the heads of deep runs and on the sides of humps and points often will have channel cats all over them.

Blues, more so than the other major catfish species, may be up off the bottom. However, they usually will still be in the lower third or so of the water column, and some will usually be on the bottom. Like channel catfish, blues typically will be in fairly large groups. The main differences are that the marks tend to be much larger, and blues are usually in the vicinity of big schools of baitfish.

Modern catfishing revolves around a good understanding of catfish behavior, forage, and habitat, specific to species and season. That knowledge, combined with ever-improving technology, gives anglers who know how to read their electronics a very good idea of what lies beneath them any given day. Now if there was only a device that could make the catfish bite!

Accessories

Like most folks, catfishermen like to have all the modern bells and whistles. Well, bells anyway. Special catfishing bells clip on rod tips to signal bites in the night.

Beyond literal bells, though, veteran catfishermen really do use a fair amount of specialized stuff. In addition to the basic tackle required for virtually all kinds of fishing, assorted items help make various styles of catfishing more efficient, comfortable, or fun.

Some are legitimate tools and are necessary for accomplishing specific tasks. Others are probably more accurately described as toys. All enhance catfishing trips in one way or another.

Lights

Because so much catfishing occurs after the sun goes down, lights of various sorts often are necessary equipment. Lighting needs begin with lights required for safe boating after hours. Angers who go out by boat at night must have proper navigation lights in good working order, and should keep them running through the night.

Beyond staying safe and legal, the most basic need that most anglers have is to simply see to do things with their hands, like tying knots, baiting hooks, and unhooking catfish. Lights that illuminate the boat would serve that purpose, but most fishermen think those types of lights attract too many bugs and have the potential to spook the fish. Plus, sitting under a spotlight takes away a bit of the unique appeal of fishing at night.

Instead, most anglers prefer localized light sources, of which every manner of hand-held or boat-mounted light has been tried by some catfisherman. Arguably, the best type of light is a strap-on headlamp. Headlamps naturally point wherever fishermen look, and they require no hands for operation.

For some fishermen, seeing lines and rod tips is also very important. Those anglers almost invariably use blacklights to illuminate tips and line. They mount blacklight lamps along their gunwales and lay their lines out in the light. White rods and fluorescent-colored rod tips and lines glow like they're lighted from within with a blacklight beam shining on them.

Landing Nets

Fishermen obviously should consider size carefully when they buy nets for the purposes of landing fish that might weigh more than 50 pounds. At the same time, it's important to consider whether a net appears to be constructed tough enough for the size of its scoop. For really large nets, the kind that big-cat specialists need, models that have collapsible handles, are more practical than others to store.

Another essential thing to remember about landing nets is that no net does a bit of good if it's tangled among ten other things in a storage compartment when a big cat is on the line. Veteran catfishermen have establish places for essential gear like landing nets, and they don't cast out the first line until everything that might be needed is in its proper place.

Bait Nets

Many styles of catfishing revolve around having fresh baitfish, and often the only way that a fisherman gets fresh bait is to catch it. Assorted traps and bait-catching rigs work for specific situations and types of bait, but most anglers rely on nets for bringing baitfish

Figure 13. A large, well-constructed net is essential gear for landing heavyweight catfish. Along with owning the right kind of net, a fisherman must keep a net in a place where it can be retrieved when it is needed.

into the boat. A few of the most popular net styles are castnets, dip-nets, and seines.

Castnets, which open into big circles when anglers throw them and are weighted to sink over schools of baitfish, are easily the most popular style of net. Major variables are net radius and mesh size. Larger castnets catch more fish, but they are more work to throw and harder to open consistently. Mesh size controls the size baitfish a net will catch.

Along with castnets, bait-style dipnets work well in many instances. Dipnets look like small landing nets except that they have small mesh for scooping up baitfish. They work great when shad or herring are shallow and corralled around some type of struc-ture, like riprap, a dam face, or a seawall. Often, anglers can scoop up shad in places where it would be very difficult to open a castnet.

Seines, which stretch vertically between posts, are most often used by catfishermen for catching stream critters, like crawfish and hellgrammite. Anglers stretch seines across swift, shallow runs, often flipping upstream rocks to get the bait stirred up. Some fishermen also seine their own minnows in shallow waters along the edges of lakes.

Net styles and sizes, mesh sizes, places where bait nets can be used and species that can be kept are all regulated in various states' game laws, so it's important to check the rules before shopping for nets.

Rod Holders

Because most catfishermen put out several lines, quality rod holders are valuable gear in boats. Beyond the fact that big cats can and sometimes do yank rods out of boats, rod holders position rods so they are out of the way but still convenient to grab.

Rod holders come in every imaginable design, and catfishermen's opinions differ widely on which work best. The two most important things about a holder are that a fish *cannot* pull out the rod and that a fisherman can get the same rod out easily. Other factors worth considering are how holders mount to boats, and how easily angles and heights can be adjusted.

Beyond rod holders that mount on boats, commercially manufactured rod holders designed for bank-fishermen work a lot better than forked sticks for keeping rods and reels in place when big cats latch on. Most have spiked ends so anglers can drive them solidly into the ground and a holder configuration that won't let rods go.

Hand Tools

Probably the most valuable hand-sized tool that a catfisherman can keep nearby is some kind of hook remover. Cats often slurp baits down, and getting hooks out can be tough, even with pliers. Assorted gadgets, all with some type of fork or grabber at the end of an extended arm, are awfully nice to have when cats get hooked deep.

Beyond hook removers, most tools that catfishermen might use are contained in good multifunction tools. Most of these tools are compact and stay out of the way in belt-loop sheaths.

Anchors and Sea Anchors

While anchors hold boats in place, sea anchors slow drifts and control the orientation of boats. Whether anchored or drifting, boat positioning is often very important to catfishing success.

Anchors come in a lot of different styles, and each has its advocates. Some grip more effectively than others, even in strong currents and with smooth bottoms, but sometimes the grabbiest anchors are also the most likely to snag in rocky or timber-filled waters. Boat size, more than anything else, dictates anchor size, but the amount of current an angler will encounter also must be taken into account.

With every anchor comes a need for anchor rope, and fishermen should get at least twice the length of rope as depth of the deepest water they intend to fish. In strong current, especially, it sometimes take a lot of scope to get an anchor to catch and hold.

Sea anchors, also called drift socks, look a lot like parachutes and they work roughly the same way, except they catch water instead of air. Anglers throw one or more sea anchors overboard to slow a boat's drift and control the boat's orientation, which keeps lines from getting crossed repeatedly.

Bait holders

Bait holders range from foam cups to large round bait tanks, which have sophisticated aeration and filtration systems. The latter are essential for keeping shad and some other baitfish alive, making them valuable to some flathead fishermen.

For most catfishing applications, basic bait buckets and coolers will do the job, but a couple specialty bait-holding devices are handy for specific applications. Little bait cubs that clip onto belts or clothing loops and have snap-on lids are great for wading streams, when hellgrammites or spring lizards need to be contained but kept within reach.

Scales

Finally, while not having a good scale won't keep a fisherman from catching a big catfish, it's a whole lot more satisfying to be able to state with certainty that a fish weighed 48 pounds, 12 ounces than to contend that it "had to weigh close to 50 pounds."

Because flatheads and blues can grow so large, catfishermen who spend days or nights on big-cat waters ought to consider buying a 100-pound scale. If a cat bottoms out that size scale, it probably needs to be taken somewhere else to be weighed on a certified scale!

Chapter 4

Catfishing Strategies

Drifting

Drift-fishermen don't like sitting around waiting for things to happen. Instead they set out looking for action. Specifically, they look for catfishing action. By covering a lot of water, drifters find the kinds of structure and the depths that hold the most cats—and the most active cats—any given day or night.

The term "drifting" sounds carefree, even random, but nothing could be farther from the truth. Most anglers who use this approach carefully consider where they want to begin each drift, and they watch their electronics tirelessly as they fish. Drift-fishermen pay attention to minute details every time a rod goes down, ever seeking to establish or tighten patterns. By day's end, they commonly know exactly what depths and types of cover they need to drift over and how fast the boat should be moving.

Drifting works best on reservoirs and on very large rivers. On southern reservoirs, drifting can be effective year 'round. On rivers, it's primarily a summertime strategy. For drifting to be effective, the cats must be somewhat spread out, and through the cool months cats really tend to "hole up" on most big rivers.

Drifting is more popular on the Santee Cooper Lakes than on any other southern reservoir, but it will work on any reservoir that has broad, open areas that blue or channel catfish cruise. A fair number of catfishermen do drift on several impoundments along the Tennessee River and on various big Texas reservoirs.

Catfish anglers in the Midwest also drift extensively, dragging chunks of coagulated blood across the bottom. Drifting blood has never gained widespread popularity in the South, but Nebraska anglers have proven in several tournaments held on southern waters, including Santee Cooper, that their style of drifting works well on southern cats.

Most Midwestern anglers use the same basic approaches as Santee drifters do. They just drag a different kind of bait. On Santee Cooper, where drifters catch blue catfish primarily, most bait up with whole or cut shad and herring of various sorts.

Most Santee Cooper drifters spend the bulk of the their time on Lake Moultrie, which is open and bowl shaped and spreads over 60,000 acres. Under the lake's expansive open body lie hills, valleys, rivers, creeks, farms, swamps, roads and much more, all flooded in the 1940s, when the lake was built.

I've drifted Santee Cooper several times, and it seems like anglers just ride to the middle of the lake, cut the engine and start fishing. In truth, their starting points are carefully considered. Guides who fish the lake daily know the areas where the most baitfish and catfish have been hanging out. Other anglers know from experience what depths and areas of the lake tend to produce best during different seasons and under various conditions.

Generally speaking, drifters like to fish over areas that have a lot of depth variances, especially early in a trip. Catfish can be quite depth-specific any given day, meaning most will hold in a certain depth range, or those cats within a given depth range will feed most actively. By drifting across hills and valleys or old creek and river channels, anglers can test a variety of depths as they go.

Some drifters do quite a bit of looking before they ever put out lines. They want to find groups of fish—or at least good concentrations of baitfish—to drift over before they start. Once they find the fish, they either triangulate with shoreline landmarks to remember where they are or punch a couple of GPS buttons to mark the area. Then they move upwind of that spot and set up to start drifting.

Most drifters use sea anchors, also called drift socks, to control the speed and the direction of their drift. They put one or more of the socks out on the side they want to fish from. The socks stay behind the boat and keep it from turning in the wind. The number of socks depends on the strength of the wind and the speed the anglers want to drift. Lacking enough wind to drift, some fishermen will turn to a different approach. Others will turn to their trolling motors and "create their own drift."

Once the boat is in position, most drifters will bait four to six lines. If the fish start biting well, even those who start with half a dozen lines out generally will drop back to four or less. Any more makes for a lot of crossed lines once the action heats up, and it doesn't typically produce more fish because there isn't time or space to handle more lines effectively.

On Santee Cooper, most anglers drift blueback herring, threadfin shad, or menhaden, depending on which are most abundant in the areas they want to fish at that time. On other waters, big pieces of cut gizzard shad or skipjack or whole threadfin shad would work better. Generally speaking, the best bait matches the kind of baitfish the big blues and channels are accustomed to seeing and eating. Where channel cats predominate, anglers who want to drift should bait up with small pieces of baitfish, chicken livers, or fairly thick dip baits.

Santee Cooper drifters like to put out a lot of line, often 50 yards or more, so the bait drags steadily across the bottom, instead of bouncing with waves. For that reason, most drifters prefer braided lines and long rods that have soft tips but plenty of backbone. The right rods and line are both important for detecting strikes a long distance away and making solid hook-sets.

Because the rigs drag across the bottom, among stumps and rocks and various other obstructions, drift rigs are designed to be as snag-free as possible. Most anglers use special weights just for drifting, but opinions vary widely on what type of weight works best for keeping the rig down but out of trouble. Some anglers use special bottom-walking weights, designed for drifting and popular with walleye fishermen. Others use lead-filled surgical tubing, while other use elongated weights with holes through them or eyes molded into one end or both ends.

With most styles of weight, anglers will run the line through the weight or its line eye and then use a swivel and piece of leader to continue rigging. For weights that have an eye on each end, the main line attaches to one eye and the leader to the other. Most fishermen put a couple feet of leader between the weight and the hook, and many add a small float, like crappie fishermen would use, six or

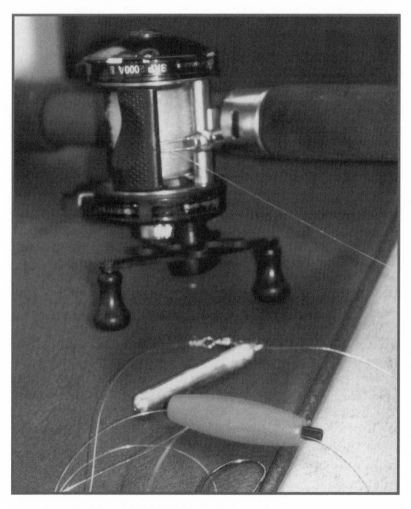

Figure 14. A popular drift-fishing rig includes a small float between the weight and the hook, which keeps the hook from dragging bottom and spares anglers a lot of snags.

eight inches from the hook. The float keeps the baited hook just barely off the bottom and saves fishermen a lot of snags.

Many river drifters, unlike their still-water counterparts, don't drag their baits. They use three-way rigs weighted with large enough bank sinkers for the line to stay almost straight below them as they drift. They reel in and let out line as they go, according to the contours of the river bottom. Where bottoms are quite sandy and obstructions are minimal, some anglers will drag their baits, still using three-way rigs, but most won't put them very far behind the boat.

Drifting heats up with the summer on big rivers as water levels stabilize. With warm water and modest flows, living conditions get very good for baitfish and catfish on open rivers. Unlike winter, when the cats must pile up in deep refuge holes, or spring, when high water pushes them into backwaters, summer brings conditions that allow the cats to spread out and feed actively.

The best areas for drifting in rivers have very uneven bottoms, with plenty of sandbars and cuts behind them. The cats cruise the tops of the bars and hold just behind them, picking off baitfish that come across the bars. Such bottoms usually occur in areas with moderated current, often in wide spots in rivers, just downstream of big bends or narrow chutes. The best bait for big cats on big rivers, most anglers agree, is cut skipjack or gizzard shad.

River drifters don't use sea anchors because current, not wind, pushes the boat. Instead, they typically keep their trolling motors down as they drift and hold the boat crosscurrent. By holding the boat perpendicular to the current, they can move closer to the shore or to the channel without altering the orientation of their drift. Most will move in and out quite a bit initially and then narrow in on the range of depths where they see the most cats or baitfish on the graph or attract the most strikes.

On lakes or rivers, drifters never stop thinking through variables. They think about wind and current and the holding depths of the fish. They look for baitfish concentrations as they drift and look for common denominators among strikes. If the fish that hit all seem to be holding atop humps or among stumps, they scour maps or think through areas they know of that have plenty of suitable humps or stumps.

Wind and current carry drifters across the surface as they drag their baits among catfish. However, no one who has spent any amount of time in drift-fishermen's boats would accuse these anglers of aimlessly drifting in the wind.

Flathead Hunting

Shortening days, cool nights, and orange dogwood leaves all suggest the same thing. It's time to do some serious scouting. After all, flathead catfish are about to get active. Through much of the South, flatheads bite best during "hunting seasons," and in many ways targeting flatheads is a lot like big-game hunting.

Unlike channels and blues, flatheads don't do a lot of moving. Once they find a spot that suits their tastes—typically with thick cover to hide in and food nearby—they tend to stay put. Therefore, if a fisherman puts his bait where there are no flatheads, chances of one coming along and finding it are relatively small.

For that reason, longtime flathead fishermen typically spend extensive amounts of time scouting before they ever put a line out. Like deer hunters walking ridges in search of trails, tracks, rubs, and scrapes, flathead fishermen cruise channel edges and the tops of holes, searching for fish—or at least for cover and structure that ought to hold the fish they hope to catch.

Moving-water anglers often aren't able to look for specific fish with their electronics. River flatheads often hold in thick shoreline cover that a fisherman wouldn't be able to cruise over and search with a graph. Also, holes on many rivers aren't deep enough to scout from overhead without spooking the catfish. Plus, really big flatheads are often solitary in river holes, leaving fishermen less fish to look for in good holes. River flathead fishermen study the holes themselves, searching out areas that have a combination of conditions they have found to attract flathead catfish in the past.

Logjams, hard bottoms, a range of depths in a small area, bends in the river, breaks in the current, and the presence of forage can all fit into the equation in moving water. Veteran fishermen look for river holes that combine several elements, and then try to identify the best spots within each hole.

On fairly large rivers, flathead specialists will scout individual holes very thoroughly, trying to figure out just where to set up. A 50-yard-long bluff along a big outside river bend might border a single deep hole, but within that hole might be several key spots.

Distinctive features—like hard breaks from the shallow side of the hole, sunken ledges off the bluff, rock piles, or tangles of trees on the bottom—are critical to locate. Dangling several baits 50 feet from key spots, even within a hole that has flatheads in it, is only a little bit better than casting the same baits onto the bank.

River anglers will often spend a long time scouting big holes from top to bottom. They'll drop floating marker buoys on areas they want to try or take careful note of shoreline features and depths so they can locate each area again. Then they'll fish each spot for an hour or two at a time. In big rivers, flathead fishermen might change positions half a dozen times in a night without ever moving to a completely different hole.

Most reservoir flathead fishermen take scouting a step farther. They attempt to locate actual flatheads on the graph, and they often won't set up until they have found several big fish holding

Figure 15. Flathead hunters typically begin with a good topographical map, if one is available. They look for key structural features that are close to major channels.

together in a single spot. Their electronics give them a bird's eye view of the areas where flatheads ought to hold, so it makes no sense to stop and fish until they find what they are looking for.

For unfamiliar waters, especially on reservoirs, the searching process ideally begins with a good topographical map. River fish by nature, flatheads continue to relate to creek and river channels, even in reservoirs. They may hold above or below a channel drop, and they often will make use of structure and cover that is not actually in the channel. However, they very rarely will roam far from a creek or river. By seeing where the rivers run, fishermen can quickly eliminate the majority of the acreage in most major reservoirs.

Beginning with major channels, fishermen will then search for unique features, like deep bends and creek confluences, and for humps or points near the channel edges. Timber stands or stump fields that stretch close to channels are likewise noteworthy, if marked on a map.

During early summer, flatheads often key on structures up river and creek arms, where some of the fish will have migrated to spawn. Through the dog days, flatheads on many lakes will use fairly shallow structure, often above ledges or shallow parts of feeder channels, because dissolved oxygen levels become too low in deeper water.

Once on the water, fishermen use maps and graphs to find and follow channel edges, looking above and below the drops for huge fish on or near the bottom that are holding close to cover. Veteran flathead fishermen spend countless hours staring at their electronics. They know from looking at an echo whether a fish is a flathead, and they usually know roughly how big the fish is. By the position of the fish, some anglers even have a pretty good idea about whether the fish are active. Generally speaking, fish that are holding just off the bottom are more active than those that are right on the bottom.

Most reservoir flathead fishermen like to find at least four big fish holding together before they put any baits in the water. Time spent searching for a good group of fish is much more wisely spent than time spent waiting with baits down in a hole that doesn't look especially good.

Almost all veteran flathead fishermen agree that a flathead prefers a good live bait. Blue cat fishermen occasionally catch hefty flatheads on cut shad or herring, but live bait is the overwhelming

No. 1 choice of anglers who target flatheads. When it comes to the question of the best kind of live bait, anglers' opinions become much more varied.

Flatheads seemingly will eat nearly any live fish, but they show preferences according to what normally shows up at the dinner table. Stomach samples have shown that smaller catfish make up a huge part of flatheads' diet in some waters.

Beyond what the flatheads like best, bait species sometimes must be selected based on a state's game laws or the kinds of fish that are most readily available. Bream, for example, are probably the single most popular kind of fish used for flathead bait in the South as a whole. However, in some states, bream are considered game fish and game fish may not be used as bait. Some flathead fishermen seek variety above all else in obtaining bait, wanting to set a buffet, so to speak, and let the flatheads pick their favorite offerings.

Flatheads generally don't like a bait that is lying directly on the bottom, so many flathead fishermen present their live baits just off the bottom. In lakes, they will anchor directly over fish they have marked, drop Carolina-rigged lines straight down, and then crank each reel handle one or two turns to get the baits a couple feet off the bottom. Some fishermen use leaders of several feet to give the baitfish plenty of room to cruise naturally.

In rivers, where currents or shallow water might make it impractical to set up right over the fish, large slip-corks are often added to each rig and used to suspend baits off the bottom in prime areas. River fishermen also will sometimes free-line a bait or two in the deep part of the hole. Other river fishermen, who don't believe they are hampered by fishing a bottom rig, use basic Carolina rigs and cast them downstream into holes.

Flathead fishermen typically put out several lines, with numbers of lines varying according to what state laws allow. Once the baits are down, the fishing again becomes like big-game hunting. More so than other kinds of catfishing, flathead fishing tends to be a big-time waiting game. As the top predators in most rivers and lakes where they live, flatheads eat what they want to and when they want to. It is not uncommon for half a dozen big fish to ignore several baits for an hour before three or four of them decide to feed almost at once.

Experience teaches anglers how long to wait on the flatheads in any given spot. How the fish have been biting in recent days, whether they are moving about in the hole, how many fish have been marked, and whether any bites have occurred all figure into the equation. Most experienced anglers won't abandon any hole without giving the fish at least 45 minutes, however, and some fishermen will wait for hours, knowing that the flatheads will bite eventually.

When flathead catfish do bite, there is seldom much question about when to set the hook. They aren't nibblers, and their strikes are seldom subtle. A rod will just start rattling in the rod holder as its tip surges toward the water, often dipping down into it.

The fish is often solidly hooked by the time an angler pries the rod out of the holder, but experienced flathead fishermen will still come up swinging, with a strong hook-set. Flatheads have very bony mouths and thick, rubbery skin, and sometimes they will pull several yards off the spool before simply letting go, having never even been hooked.

Figuring out where flathead catfish ought to be, scouting out such spots, setting up and then waiting for the fish to decide to bite requires too much effort to then miss the fish by not setting the hook. As thrilling as a jarring flathead bite is, the deal is not sealed until the fish is flopping in the net.

Again, flathead fishing is like big-game hunting. As thrilling as it is to even spot a big buck, it's hard to go home fully satisfied if something goes awry and sends the deer scampering away without even the opportunity for a killing shot having been afforded.

Tailwater Fishing

When Jerry Crook gave the word, we dropped our three-way rigs toward the bottom. Current raced past us on both sides of the boat, but we were positioned in a mid-river eddy, which existed because the turbine immediately upstream was not running. Our large cut-shad offerings fell to the bottom of a deep hole, which had been scoured out by currents from the same turbine. It was an ideal tailwater catfish hole, and in a moment, three bent and bouncing rods provided the evidence.

Tailwaters, which are the river sections immediately down-stream of hydroelectric dams, definitely rank among the hottest spots in many river systems throughout the South for catfish. Dams block migration routes of catfish and baitfish alike, creating big concentrations of fish. At the same time, most provide abundant rocky cover at a good range of depths, plus good currents, which make fish more active and define feeding areas.

Most tailwaters are also accessible to bank-fishermen, either from riprap banks or from some kind of casting platform. Where boating access is restricted within a certain distance of a dam, in fact, bank-fishermen may actually enjoy better access to prime catfish waters than is available to anglers in boats.

Tailwaters come in every imaginable size and configuration. Dams along many small streams have only one or two turbines. Meanwhile dams that impound major rivers, like the Tennessee or Arkansas River, have numerous turbines for power generation, spill gates for water-level control, and locking systems that are big enough to accommodate barges. Big dams are extremely complex, but they offer the best overall prospects for big numbers of high-quality cats because of the sheer amount of habitat they offer and the normal abundance of food.

Jerry Crook, a full-time fishing guide from Gardendale, Alabama, does almost all of his fishing within sight of Wheeler and Wilson dams, huge dams on the Tennessee River. Both are daunting, with numerous turbines and spill gates, plus twin sets of locks. River conditions, including the amount of water racing over rocky hazards, pushiness and directions of currents, and the catfish's behavior and holding areas, vary enormously from day to day. In fact, conditions often vary hourly, according to which turbines are "on" and which are off and whether any spill gates are open.

Some catfish can be caught from tailwaters year 'round, and on some rivers, spring fishing is outstanding, largely because of baitfish runs. However, Crook's best catfishing typically kicks off around early June, which is when a lot of the catfish in the Tennessee River have finished spawning. Good fishing typically continues through the end of September or October.

The tailwaters that Jerry Crook focuses on offer all three major catfish species in good numbers and sizes. Crook targets each

Figure 16. Tailwaters provide abundant food, current, and cover for catfish, and often hold big concentrations of cats. Jerry Crook, a tailwater guide on the Alabama portion of the Tennessee River, hoists a couple of nice blues.

differently, deciding what to go after based on water conditions, what the fish have been doing in recent days and weeks, and his clients' preferences.

Fishing for blue cats is best, by far, when some turbines are on and others are off. Blues feed more aggressively when some water is moving, but they don't like to fight the powerful direct currents downstream of running turbines. Crook likes to have gaps of one to three "off" turbines between those that are running. That creates upstream currents circling back into the gaps and well-defined seams between current lines, which cats often lie directly under.

Prime zones include the washout holes below any turbines that aren't running, seams at the edges of main currents, and submerged rockpiles and deep holes within a couple hundred yards of the dam. Rockpiles produce best when fairly strong currents are pushing directly over them.

Crook generally baits up for blues with fresh threadfin shad, which he catches with a dipnet or castnet. The shad may be whole or cut, depending on their size and the size of cats he is targeting. Cut skipjack also make great blue catfish bait in tailwaters, and sometimes they are available when shad are not. If skipjack are breaking the surface in swift water, a small white or chartreuse jig (or better yet, two or three small jigs) will usually get one in the boat in short order.

Crook fishes vertically, using three-way rigs, pegged with one to three ounces of weight. Keeping his tiller-controlled outboard running all the time, he starts with the boat over the upstream end of the zone he expects the fish to be holding in and either holds position or lets the boat drift. Either way, boat positioning and control are always critical.

While there are basic patterns that major currents follow, based on which turbines are on, water appears to be going every direction most of the time. Anglers must learn to "read" tailwaters and figure out where the fish should be. They also must learn how to operate a boat in the strong, multidirectional currents.

In Crook's boat, anglers drop their offerings to the bottom with baitcasting gear and then reel up or let out line as needed to keep it ticking but not dragging the bottom. "If it stays on the bottom long, it'll get hung for sure," Crook warns anglers. However, if the bait is too far up from the bottom it probably won't get bit.

If a bait stays near the bottom but not quite on it, it usually isn't long before something latches on. When the bait is a big piece of cut shad, the fish that grabs it is likely to be a blue catfish. All bets are off when a hook gets set in a big-river tailwater, though. The fish at the other end could be a flathead or channel catfish instead, or it could be a striper, hybrid, drum, buffalo, bass, or something else.

When he targets channel catfish, Crook again focuses on the washout holes near the dam. However, he prefers to have several adjacent turbines turned off so there are fewer swirling currents. He generally uses the same rigs, with just an ounce or so of weight for the less turbulent water.

Crook baits up with chicken livers, which he brings numerous containers of, for channel cats. Once the catfish get below Wilson and Wheeler dams in big numbers, chicken livers don't stay in the strike zone for an instant without getting nabbed. Crook doesn't catch many big really fish on livers, but the action typically is outstanding.

For flatheads, Crook moves to the slack water and fishes around large structural features along the dam. The spill gates, assuming they are not running, the sides of the lock structures, and the rock jetties that divide sections of the tailwater all offer good prospects. Along those features, he likes the deepest water available.

Crook sticks with three-way rigs for flathead fishing, but his approach is much less active. It's more of a waiting game. Each angler puts down one line, rigged with a big, live threadfin shad, and suspends the bait with the weight just off the bottom. Then it's just a matter of waiting on the flatheads to bite.

While fishing for blues and channels is definitely best through the dog days, Crook catches more flatheads during the fall than through the summer. Beginning some time during September each year, he will begin hearing of flatheads being caught—usually by striper fishermen using big live baits. That's when he'll start doing some flathead fishing. Once they start biting well, the flatheads usually continue to offer good fishing through October and sometimes into November.

For all three species, Crook matches medium-heavy Shakespeare Ugly Stik Graphite rods with Medalist reels, which he spools up with 17-pound-test Excalibur line. He has tried heavier line, but found it too difficult to break battling strong currents when lines get snagged. He will go a bit heavier for flatheads, where fishing is more stationary and snags are far less frequent and problematic.

Most tailwaters are far smaller and less complex than the two that Jerry Crook fishes. Many have only a handful of generators, of which one or two often will be running. Again, the best areas for channels and blues generally will be close to but not right in the strongest currents.

If there's just one turbine running, with a well-defined seam on each side of the main current line, those seams generally will hold most of the fish. Beyond that, the key is to find the best spots along those seams, which may be in deep holes, behind big boulders, or over rockpiles.

It's worth noting that dams often affect river fishing for many miles downstream. When any dam is running close to its full potential, whether that means one turbine or 20, the waters immediately below the dam are likely to be virtually washed out and too swift for catfishing. Under such conditions, more traditional river holes several miles downstream will be far easier to set up over than waters immediately below the dam, and they typically will yield terrific fishing.

Rockpiles, wing dikes, or other large, physical obstructions that form major eddies can also hold big piles of cats when tailwaters are running a lot of water. Using the same tight-line setups that Crook uses close to the dam, fishermen can sometimes catch fish after fish from a single spot.

Arguably more so than any other type of waterway, tailwaters demand extreme caution. Powerful currents and sometimes turbulent waters can smash boats against structure or even flip them, and water levels can rise or drop several feet in a hurry. Turbines, which are sometimes opened without warning, can create huge boils. Meanwhile, rockpiles and other hazards sometimes lie hidden in very shallow water. Fishermen drown in tailwaters every year.

On popular tailwaters, other fishermen create the biggest hazards. Numerous boaters using a single section of river can cause problems for one another, especially when some are drifting and others are anchored. Fishermen must give one another space, especially close to the dam, where currents are the strongest and least predictable.

Anglers should heed all posted safety warnings, wear life jackets where required (and beyond, as seems prudent), stay on the lookout for hazards and other boaters, and study the dynamics of tailwaters under various conditions. Finally, while anglers commonly do so, tying a boat to any dam face is asking for trouble.

Night-Fishing

Staring at fluorescent rod tips, made to glow by a blacklight beam, two anglers sit waiting for things that go bump in the night. They talk about everything and nothing as they anticipate one of the glow-in-the-dark tips surging suddenly toward the water's dark surface. They're fishing after-hours because they have found that the night bite is better once summer sets in.

All of the South's popular catfish species are at least somewhat nocturnal, with flatheads being more tuned into the nighttime hours than their cousins. Through the summer, even more so than the rest of the year, most cats feed more actively through the night than during the day.

In addition to the better bite that tends to occur beneath starry skies, the setting of the sun sends the daily barrage of pleasure boaters home, which makes catfishing far more enjoyable. As importantly, summer nights feel far more pleasant than summer days throughout the South. Even when dog-day cats will bite, the mid-afternoon sun sometimes can be almost unbearable on the open water.

In many ways, night-fishing for catfish is not much different from daytime fishing. Big blues still like chunks of cut bait, flatheads still prefer live fish, and channels are still quick to sample various stinky offerings. The same rods and reels meet the task in various waterways, as do the same basic types of rigs.

From a fishing-approach standpoint, the biggest difference between day-fishing and night-fishing is that the cats tend to move up out of the deep holes to feed on nearby flats after hours. They still relate to the same kinds of holes. They just cruise the edges of the holes instead of holding down in the deep water. Often cats will start the night fairly deep, and then work their way shallower as the hours pass.

From a practical standpoint, the biggest differences between fishing during the day or through the night have to do with the simple fact that the world is dark at night. Strategies sometimes need to be altered not because the fish behave differently but because of limitations related to access and presentations.

Through the day, for example, fishermen often move quite frequently until they locate actively feeding cats. If the fish don't bite,

Figure 17. Catfish move shallower and generally become more active at night, especially during the summer. The author caught this blue from near the edge of a creek channel on cut skipjack.

it's rarely a big deal to move to another hole or at least to reposition the boat within a hole and spread baits over different depths or around different types of cover.

After hours, moving often becomes impractical. At times, it's impossible. On many rivers, changing locations after dark would be treacherous. In other instances, getting down the river might not present a problem, but setting up properly in a new spot would be next to impossible without the benefit of having daylight to see current lines and clumps of cover and other features that affect setups.

Even on lakes and reservoirs, where it's often fairly easy to move from one location to another, finding new spots and setting up to fish them can be difficult at night unless an angler is already quite familiar with specific areas.

Whether on rivers or lakes, often the key to nighttime success is thorough daytime scouting. Again, depending on the practicality of after-hours travel, anglers might scout hard to find the single premium spot and learn everything they can about it or try to pick out a handful of potentially productive catfish holes that could be explored over the course of a night.

Beyond identifying holes they expect to have catfish in them, anglers scouting for a night of fishing must give serious consideration to probable setups and potential problems. They have to consider how they might shift their position if the cats would not cooperate and figure out how they would find that position without the benefit of shoreline landmarks.

Whether they plan to move a few times during the night or pick a spot and stay put, most fishermen like to wrap up their scouting before the sun gets too low so they can be in position and have their baits in place by sunset. The final hour or so of daylight, whether technically considered nighttime or not, often serves up very good catfishing. Plus, by fishing a while before it is fully dark, anglers can see whether their setup creates any problems that they did not anticipate.

Anglers who drift for cats are the exceptions to the daytime scouting/nighttime fishing pattern. Day or night, they never stop moving. They pick large open areas where they can drift for an hour or more without running into anything. Following common catfish behavior, drifters generally begin around dark by fishing the deepest waters they expect to encounter cats in and then work shallower through the night.

Because drifters move to general areas they want to fish and then let the breeze carry them, starting anew several times in a night doesn't present the same practical difficulties as it does for still-fishermen, who often must set up in precise positions. In fact, with modern electronic units, many of which include GPS technology, some drifters are just about as well acclimated at night as they are during the day.

Once they start fishing, neither drifters nor anglers who set up on spots alter their approach significantly after hours, except for fishing shallower, overall, and possibly staying in spots longer. There are some differences in gear requirements, however. Again, most differences relate to the simple fact that it is harder to see at night.

Assuming they have a good idea of where they can and cannot cast, the most important things for anglers to see are their hands when they do things like tying knots and baiting hooks. For various reasons, most anglers don't like to illuminate the whole boat. Some believe that doing so can spook fish, especially if the cats are shallow, and staring into lights limits anglers' abilities to watch rod tips or see other stuff around them. Also, lights tend to attract insects on southern nights.

Most fishermen prefer localized light sources, and probably no type of light suits catfishing better than a little head lamp, like a cave explorer would use. Such a light points wherever a fisherman looks, with no hands required. Some headlamps are even water-proof and float.

Beyond seeing to do things in the boat, anglers sometimes need to keep a close eye on their lines or rod tips. That's not a big concern for fishermen targeting jumbo blues or flatheads. They sim-ply wait for clickers to start screaming or for rods to start rattling in holders. In fact, big-cat specialists who trust the fish to hook them-selves commonly stretch out in the bottom of the boat and let the bite serve as an alarm clock!

Not all catfish bite quite so abruptly, however, so many anglers use white rods, which are easier to see at night than darker ones. Others use rods that have fluorescent tips and spool up with fluores-cent line. They run all their lines out of one side of the boat and use a side-mounted blacklight lamp to make their rod tips and lines glow.

Equipment related, nighttime anglers ought not forget a wind-breaker or sweatshirt—even in the middle of the summer in the South. Also, with or without lights shining in the boat all night, bug spray is indispensable on some nights. Related to lights, proper nighttime navigation lights should be left running through the night for the sake of legality and safety.

As for the best time of the night to fish, the catfishing jury remains fairly evenly divided. Some would point toward the wee-est of wee hours as being the best of the best. Others contend that dusk and dawn bring the better fishing than the middle of the night. Still others would contend that the best time varies by night, based on the phase of the moon, among other factors.

Regarding the moon, anglers are again divided on the best nights to fish. Days immediately prior to and after the full moon would probably get the most votes, but many anglers would go the opposite direction and point toward the new moon. Whenever the catfish bite best, fishing certainly is easier on nights when the moon shines brightly.

Of course, the best night to go catfishing, as far as I am concerned, is any night a buddy and I can break away and can afford to forsake a night's sleep.

Wading

An angler plopped down on a bucket, staring at rods propped on forked sticks, is a classic catfishing image, as is that of a couple of anglers sitting comfortably in boat seats and watching a bevy of rods set in holders. Less familiar to most catfishermen is the notion of wading up a stream and casting to cats while standing in the water among them.

As unfamiliar as the approach is, however, wading proves good means for accessing excellent catfish waters. As significantly, wading is simply a fun way to go after cats, especially during the summer. Anglers stand in the catfish's hallways and cast baits right into the fish's dining rooms. Tackle and techniques are basic, and the cool water feels good on a toasty summer day.

Catfish abound in small to medium-sized streams throughout the South, and countless miles of those streams get very little attention from catfishermen. Long sections of many streams are too small, shallow, or swift for most boats, and shoreline access is commonly limited to a handful of spots. Those waters are unfishable by boat or by bank, but anglers who don't mind getting wet and walking a little can move from hole to hole, enjoying outstanding catfishing and little to no company.

Beyond creeks, a lot of lakes actually lend themselves nicely to the wading approach. Wading opens up a lot of waters to anglers who don't own boats, yet very few anglers ever step out into a lake to fish. Extensive flats on many lakes have hard, sandy bottoms that can be traveled on foot, often to within casting distance of productive channel edges. Boatless anglers who stay on the bank severely limit the waters they are able to reach in many instances.

Wading fishermen must keep their gear simple because they have to carry everything they will need in a day. Normal tackle

Figure 18. Wading is a very effective and vastly underutilized method for accessing prime catfish waters. Mike Wilson used a live hellgrammite to pull this nice channel from a hole beneath a shoal on the Pigeon River.

consists of a light spinning outfit, a bait container of some kind, a tool or two for tasks like unhooking fish, and a stowable tackle box loaded with hooks, small weights, and possibly a couple of corks.

Necessary gear for a normal day fits neatly in fishing vest pockets or even in large shirt pockets. Anglers who also like to carry lunch or a first-aid kit or who prefer to have a few more tackle options might want to tote their stuff in a backpack or fanny pack.

As for wading gear, jeans and tennis shoes will work, but light-weight, quick-drying pants are a lot more comfortable than soggy jeans, and felt-bottomed wading shoes prevent anglers from slipping in streams that have rocky bottoms. While chest waders make catfish waters wadable throughout the seasons, the best catfishing in most small streams and lake flats occurs from late spring through mid-fall. Unless an angler simply wants to stay dry, wading wet is generally a more practical and enjoyable option.

Often, wading anglers like to catch their own bait with a seine or other form of net. Most will gather their bait upon arrival and then tuck their nets in the woods before venturing upstream or across flats to fish. Other anglers like to set traps for crawfish or minnows. Those anglers either will make an extra trip beforehand, just to set their traps, or they will set their traps upon arrival and then fish for a while with some kind of store-bought bait while the traps do their work.

In small streams, the best catfish bait is often whatever can be caught from that particular stream. Stream fishermen will seine swift rocky runs for hellgrammites, crawfish, and other small critters, or seine grass-lined backwater areas for minnows and other small forage fish. Flipping rocks will also produce various critters that make good catfish bait.

For lake fishing, threadfin shad, minnows, and other small baitfish that cruise flats make great bait. Anglers often walk the flats with small castnets and watch for flipping shad. They might then put the baitfish in a bucket, tied to a belt loop, or just put them in a bait cup or plastic bag. Unless they are targeting flatheads, most catfishermen don't worry about keeping baitfish alive anyway.

Other popular baits with wading anglers include night crawlers, which are often dug up from beside the stream, crickets, or chicken livers. Whatever the bait, most anglers stay very simple with their rigs. If a hook and a split shot will get a bait down to the bottom, that's all most wading angler like to rig up with. If needed, they might go to light Carolina rigs or use rubber-core sinkers.

Some anglers actually prefer to free-line natural offerings. The only downside, at least to catfishing purists, is that bass and various other kinds of fish sometimes make it difficult to get a crawfish or a night crawler down to the catfish.

In streams, prime waters to probe for catfish typically are fairly obvious. Any hole that's deeper than the rest of the stream is apt to hold a few cats, and the bigger the hole, the better its offerings usually are. Of course, while classic holes on outside bends usually deserve the most attention, anglers also shouldn't overlook short, deep runs along undercut banks, especially if they cut under logs or overhanging bushes. Stream cats don't need super-deep water if they have good, dense cover to hide in.

Anglers should expect mostly channel catfish and bullheads from most southern streams that are small enough to wade. However, live bait will produce occasional small flatheads, especially from big holes that have a lot of cover in them. Jumbo flatheads are rare in small streams, and they won't usually eat a hellgrammite or a crawfish, but even an 8- or 10-pound flathead will put up an absolutely fierce fight on the fairly light tackle that wading anglers typically use.

The amount of stream an angler covers in a day depends largely on the size of the stream. On very small creeks, bouncing a bait across the bottom of a hole a time or two pretty well reveals whether anyone is home. On larger streams, individual holes offer plenty of water to fish for an hour or more.

On some big streams, the best approach actually combines wading and boating. Anglers use canoes to get across stream sections that are too deep or too swift to wade through but beach the boats around all the best-looking deep runs and fish those thoroughly by wading.

The best areas for lake fishermen to key on are sometimes defined simply by the limits of where the anglers are able to wade comfortably. Experienced waders don't just step out randomly, though. They look for distinctive features, like points and creek mouths, which allow them to fish along slopes to deeper water and even put baits down in the deep water.

Where possible, wading anglers work along the edges of creek channels. A good topographical map is helpful for identifying areas that stay shallow enough wade out to channel edges. Lacking a map, shoreline topography sometimes reveals where flats will extend, and channels may be marked with buoys or recognizable by water color changes.

Cats won't always be in the deep water, however, especially if a flat has good cover on it. Therefore, anglers should be careful not to wade right past the best spots in a quest to get farther from the bank. Fallen trees and cypress knees often have catfish beside them, and on cover-rich flats, anglers can sometimes wade from tree to tree, picking catfish off almost every one.

Along a flat or in a creek, going waist-deep creates a lot of opportunities for many catfishermen.

Approaching River Holes

"We missed the spot," Tom Evans announced, having just figured out the answer to an unspoken question he'd been mulling over. We were set up to fish Evans' "Over 50 Hole," from which he has pulled several blue catfish that topped the 50-pound mark, but we weren't getting bites from fish of any size.

The hole, formed by a split in the inundated channel of the Tennessee River, sets mid-river and isn't recognizable from the surface. Evans, a longtime fishing guide, had located the hole with his graph and set up with the boat atop the lip, at the head of the hole—or so he thought.

We were anchored over only five feet of water, but the hole is close to 50 feet deep. Evans had brought in a line to replace the bait and cast it back out when he noticed something he had not observed initially. The bait didn't sink long enough before it hit bottom. We were fishing beside the hole, not in it.

We had only missed the mark by a few yards, in a section of river that was a few hundred yards wide, but that was all it took. We cranked in the other lines and pulled both anchors, and Evans went to work repositioning the boat. Within ten minutes of getting the lines back out, one was off to the races with a 30-pound blue running full stream.

Veteran river fishermen know the importance of setting up properly to fish holes. Time and again, bait shop owners or other local anglers will suggest just fishing big holes, easily recognizable by bluff banks or the wing dikes that scour out some holes. However, big holes on major rivers often encompass entire bends and may be several

Figure 19. A proper setup is important for fishing river holes. Anglers must position themselves so that they can spread offerings over the range of depths that is most apt to hold fish.

hundred yards long. Catfishermen must consider a host of factors that affect catfish locations and behavior and then set up accordingly.

For starters, every river hole is unique, and all holes change in character any time a river goes up or down, even a little bit. The best setup for any given hole also varies by season and time of day and according to the species of cat that an angler hopes to catch. Good setups must begin with an understanding of catfish behavior.

Evans, for example, fishes mostly for big blue catfish, and he does his fishing by day. Therefore, he typically wants most of his baits down in a hole or right on the slope. He often will set up right at the head of a hole initially and vary the lengths of his casts so some baits settle down in the deep water and others land on the upper-end slope. He will pay close attention to which baits get hit and adjust the lengths of subsequent casts to put as many baits as possible among the most active cats.

Once Evans believes he has done all the damage he can in a spot, he generally moves downstream within the same hole and sets up in a new spot. Most Tennessee River holes are plenty large to fish from several different points. In fact, an angler could easily fish all day, moving periodically, without ever abandoning a single hole.

Depending on how dramatically the hole drops off on the bluff side, Evans might set up close to the bluff or across the hole, on the open-river side. Either way, he will set up directly over a slope, so that with all lines stretched downstream, those at one end of the boat will be deeper than those at the other end. That allows him to continue testing a range of depths, and it puts all his baits on the slope and just above and/or below it, where cats tend to concentrate.

If Evans has clients aboard who have a special interest in flatheads, he will position the boat tight to the bluff, along a section where the drop-off is severe and where tangles of downed trees stretch into the hole. He will suspend some baits close to the treetops, drop others almost to the bottom along the bluff, and lay a couple of others out, on the bottom, downstream of the boat.

Evans would set up differently if he were to fish the same holes under the stars. Because catfish tend to move out of big holes to feed over adjacent flats at night, he would position the boat a cast's length upstream of the main drop or along the edge of a hole. He might still put a couple baits on the slope, but most would be up on the flat, instead of down in the hole.

For Evans, slope and depth largely dictate where he sets up within a hole. For James Patterson, a Mississippi River guide, current dictates where he will set up, more so than any other single factor. Big holes in the Mississippi, whether behind dikes or along riverbends, are full of ups and downs because of circling currents that continually rearrange the sandy bottom. Depth gradients, therefore, are almost a given for Patterson, and he can usually find whatever depths he needs.

However, those same big circling currents create vast dead zones, where there is little to no current or where the direction of the current is highly variable. Without steady current, Patterson cannot anchor his boat and lay his lines out the way he prefers. Also, while fish pile up in slack areas of big holes, those fish are generally inactive and very tough to catch. Patterson looks for groups of fish beneath good current lines and anchors his boat upcurrent of the fish.

Whether an angler seeks deep water, shallow water, thick cover, or steady current, setting up on a hole begins with examining the hole carefully. Except in very small rivers where a look from the surface reveals virtually all there is to learn about a hole, most veteran catfishermen will do a fair amount of looking with their electronics before they ever drop an anchor.

They want to know a hole's length and shape, the locations of its deepest spots and sharpest drops, what kind of cover it hides and where baitfish and catfish are holding. It's not uncommon for serious big-river catfishermen to spend half an hour or more studying a single hole before they start fishing. Some will even predetermine several specific spots they want to try.

Patterson and Evans both like to anchor their boats upstream of where they expect the most cats to be and cast all lines downstream. Patterson uses only a front anchor, letting the boat rest parallel to the current. As long as the current is strong and steady, the boat sways very little that way. He typically puts out two or three lines on each side, varying the lengths of his casts to cover the most water.

Evans prefers to use two anchors in order to position the boat perpendicular to the current. By doing so, he can spread out several lines and keep an eye on them all, as all are on the same side of the boat. He angles his front and back lines out, but casts the rest pretty much straight downstream.

Double anchoring calls for a lot of scope in the ropes, both upstream and away from the boat. Evans drops one anchor upstream of and toward the bank from where he wants to fish, lets it catch, and then moves back upstream but on the opposite side of his target position to drop the other anchor. Once both anchors have caught, he takes in or lets out rope as needed to get the boat perpendicular to the current and in the right position.

With one or two anchors, positioning a boat over a specific spot in strong current requires practice. An important starting point is making good mental note of where the boat needs to end up by lining up shoreline markers in more than one direction. Having two people working together also helps enormously. One person drops the anchors and handles the lines while the other runs the boat and considers positioning.

Even veteran catfishermen commonly have to make two or three attempts before they get the boat settled where they want it. Poor positioning creates a huge handicap for fishing a river hole, so it's well worth the time and effort to pull anchor and try again, when needed.

At times, of course, currents, water depths, or obstructions make it impossible to put a boat where it really ought to be in order to deliver baits where they need to be. That's when fishermen have to become more creative with their setups. Where flathead specialists cannot set up over prime lies, for example, they often turn to slip corks, side planers, and other specialized tools to complete their setup.

Whatever tackle or tactics it take to get baits where they need to be, good setups on river holes rarely just happen. Anglers must look at what a hole has to offer, consider where the cats are apt to concentrate, and figure out the best way to put some catfish snacks in that part of the hole.

Tight-Lining

Neither rod holders nor anchors figure into the equation when Glenn Stubblefield goes catfishing. A longtime Kentucky Lake fishing guide, Stubblefield opts for an active approach. He assigns one rod per angler, which the anglers never put down while fishing, and keeps the boat moving.

Stubblefield stays busy from start to finish. Beyond re-rigging broken lines, unhooking catfish, and handing out minnows, he sometimes mans a rod and he never strays far from his trolling motor. Facing the boat upstream in the sometimes-strong currents, he uses his foot-controlled motor to keep the boat over stump-laden ridges and other "catty-looking" structure along the old channel of the Tennessee River.

Stubblefield's catfishing strategy allows him to thoroughly work areas of prime structure. It also allows him to keep minnows, which he has found to be the best bait for this approach, just off the bottom, where hungry blue and channel catfish are most likely to find them.

Heavy currents in the areas Stubblefield fishes call for constant attention to the trolling motor; however, those same currents stack

Figure 20. Glenn Stubblefield (left) uses a tight-line approach to seek out active cats along the main river channel in Kentucky Lake.

up the fish and make their locations predictable. Meanwhile, ever-changing bottom contours atop the best catfish structure demand that anglers' offerings be continually raised and lowered.

Kentucky Lake is 184 miles long and covers more than 163,000 surface acres in Tennessee and Kentucky. That's a lot of water to find catfish in, even in fertile waters that are loaded with cats. Stubblefield shortens the playing field significantly by confining his fishing to the lower third of the lake and sticking with the main Tennessee River portion. Within that area, he looks for the right combination of bottom structure, cover, and current.

"You see a lot of water out here," he said, "but you won't see me fish very much of it."

Major bends in the inundated river channel, points that stretch out toward the channel edge, and noteworthy humps rising from otherwise flat sections of river bottom provide the kind of structure that Stubblefield seeks. Prime cover comes in the form of stump fields, flooded historic home sites and fence rows, old ponds and other remnants of what used to set along the river's banks.

Current pushes through the main body of Kentucky Lake whenever water is being run through Pickwick and Kentucky dams, at the upper and lower ends of the lake, respectively. Volume varies radically, as both dams have numerous generators and spill gates, any number of which can be on at any given time.

During periods of low flow, Stubblefield is forced to do all his fishing on the upstream sides of islands and within narrow cuts and various other bottlenecked areas where some current remains. When the river is running hard, he has more places to pick from than he could fish in a month.

"The catfish are much more active in flowing water, and the stronger the current, the better," Stubblefield said. "Sometimes, when they turn on the water at one of the dams, it's just like flipping a switch. The catfish start feeding like crazy."

Stubblefield's active approach allows him to work his way through areas that offer good combinations of fish-attracting features. All the elements need not be in a single spot, as they ideally should be for still-fishing techniques, because Stubblefield works entire areas instead of specific holes. By moving gradually as he fishes, Stubblefield can cover all the features in an area and then let bites show him where the most active cats are concentrated.

Stubblefield uses a three-way rig, with a 1-ounce bell sinker at the end of a 1-foot leader and a No. 1 hook on a 6-inch leader. His bait of choice is a big crappie minnow, which he threads on the hook, through the minnow's eye and out its side. He seeks to create a good bend in the baitfish, so it will spin in the current.

Stubblefield coaches anglers to keep the line tight. The weight should bump the bottom, but not drag across it. "Barely bump the bottom with the sinker," Stubblefield said. "Otherwise, snags eat up more lines than catfish do."

With each angler holding a rod—reeling in and letting out line as needed—Stubblefield uses the trolling motor to slowly crawl against the current. Often he follows the edge of a drop or works across a stump-laden hump, never taking his eye off the depth finder as he covers every dip and knob. He take note of cats on the graph, but is more interested in finding the best structure and cover. If those elements are right, the cats aren't far away, he has learned.

While he will work every inch of a structure any time the cats cooperate, Stubblefield won't stay in an area long if the fish don't bite. There are just too many good spots on Kentucky Lake to waste time waiting for a particular bunch of catfish to get fired up.

Newcomers to Stubblefield's style of fishing tend to hook a lot of stumps. With the boat always moving, bumping a stump often feels like a fish is hitting the bait. That leads to some pretty solid hook-sets into wood, Stubblefield noted.

Veteran tight-liners learn to recognize the feel of the stumps and they finesse baits over the top of the cover, preparing themselves for hits that often follow. Cats hold tight to stumps, and when a bait slides across a stump and slips off it, a cat often will pounce on it.

Strikes often feel like nothing more than extra weight on the line, and the bigger the fish the softer the hit, in many cases. "Big fish never hit the bait hard," Stubblefield said. "They just start moving off, pulling the rod down slowly as they go."

Blue catfish comprise the bulk of Stubblefield's catch, with channel cats next in line, and flatheads showing up only on occasion. Stubblefield noted that blues and channels are quick to jump on baits that look interesting. Flatheads are a lot moodier. They like to watch baits for a long time and mull over them. They also favor big, lively meals.

Stubblefield has caught blues weighing up to 65 pounds with his tight-line method, but fish in the 5- to 15-pound range make up the bulk of his catch. Even these "smaller" cats put up very good fights on his standard tight-line outfit, an Ambassadeur 5500 reel spooled with 20-pound-test line and matched with medium-action baitcasting rod.

While Stubblefield concentrates on the impounded waters of Kentucky Lake, his method also works well for river cats. Anywhere catfish hold tight to well-defined structure that has current pushing across it and the water is deep enough to fish from overhead is a prime zone for tight-line catfishing.

Chumming

Sort of like running full-page newspaper ads prior to a big department store sale, chumming attracts crowds from all around an area—only they're crowds of catfish, instead of crowds of shoppers.

Chumming, simplified, refers to putting some type of food or fish attractant in an area where a person intends to fish. The idea is to draw fish from a broader area than the scent of the bait might reach, to concentrate the fish and, in some cases, to fire them up a bit. Chumming can be a long-term or short-term proposition and can be done in a variety of ways. Essentially, though, all anglers who chum seek the same end result of shortening the time between strikes.

Despite being an extremely effective way to increase success rates, chumming has never gained tremendous popularity among freshwater fishermen. Saltwater anglers commonly grind baitfish and put out "chum slicks" to draw in fish or get them active. Catfish, being scent and taste feeders, are prime candidates for the use of chumming strategies in fresh water.

Commercial catfishermen understand the value of chumming. They will commonly set out slowly dissolving chum a week or more before setting lines or traps in an area. If fact, some commercial anglers will keep favored areas chummed all the time and run lines regularly in those areas.

It would be tough to pinpoint exactly why chumming has never gained much popularity among catfishermen. Many fishermen probably have never given the tactic much thought, simply because they have never been taught about it. Others probably either don't know how to chum or they consider it too much work—one more step in the process that they would prefer to skip. Some fishermen, especially tournament fishermen, might think of chumming as cheating, as it is almost never permitted in catfish tournaments.

Along the lines of tournament rules, game laws relating to chumming vary substantially from state to state. In some places, chumming is illegal. In others, laws dictate how chumming can and cannot be done. Other states list no prohibitions against the practice. Therefore, a state fishing regulations digest is the best starting place for any chumming plans.

Most chumming takes on one of two basic forms: short-term and long-term. Short-term chumming typically is done within a few hours of the start of a fishing trip or even immediately prior to the first lines being cast out. It uses a heavy dose of strong, meaty scent

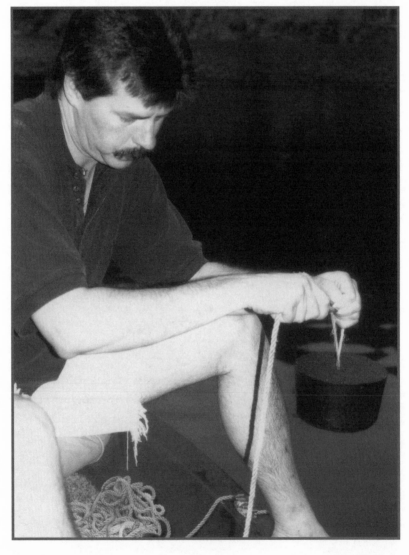

Figure 21. Chum blocks are designed to dissolve slowly, attracting baitfish and catfish to an area.

to bring cats into an area. Long-term chumming, which is what commercial catfishermen typically do, uses slowly dissipating food-stuff to attract all kinds of critters to a certain areas, using the entire food chain to bring in the cats.

For many catfishermen, short-term chumming has more practical applications than the long-term approach. Chum can be put out on the day of a fishing trip, even upon selecting a spot. Many anglers travel sufficiently far to catfishing spots that making an extra trip just to set chum often wouldn't be possible, let alone practical. Additionally, conditions often dictate which specific spots anglers should fish, especially on large rivers or lakes, and long-term chumming locks anglers into the areas they have chummed.

The best chum for the short-term approach breaks up fairly quickly in the water and puts out a lot of scent and particles. Good possibilities include chopped-up or ground-up baitfish, chicken parts, and coagulated blood. Some commercial chumming products are also designed specifically for short-term applications.

The biggest difference between catfish and most saltwater species that anglers commonly chum for is that catfish feed on or near the bottom. Saltwater fishermen simply chop or grind up fish and toss everything overboard. Catfishermen must get their chum down. They also need something that will keep the bulk of the chum under the boat, but allow enough pieces to escape to attract the fish.

Most fishermen use either a mesh or burlap bag or a 5-gallon bucket with holes drilled on it. Tied to a rope, a bag or a bucket filled with chum can be hung off to the side of the boat. Another good strategy is to sink the chum line in a high-percentage spot and then tie the rope to a jug. That allows anglers to leave the chum and let it work for a couple of hours. It also makes it possible to position the boat a cast's length from the chum and put baits all around it.

Short-term chumming naturally works best in areas that have current pushing through them. The current spreads the good-smelling stuff downstream to reach the most cats. Even in fairly strong current, which carries food particles well downstream, the scent trail gets stronger closer to the chum, and cats will "follow their whiskers" in search of the source.

It's worth noting that the advantage of having current does not limit chumming to river-fishing applications. Most southern lakes are actually impoundments, and many have current running through them much of the time. Also, while current adds to the effectiveness of chumming, it is not a necessary ingredient. The chum will still spread in slack water. It will just spread more slowly and in a less targeted fashion.

Anglers always must take into account where the slick from their chum will spread in order to put the chum in position to call up the most cats. As an example, the head of long hole along a riverbend is far better than the middle or lower section of the same hole. From the upper end, the chum can spread through the entire hole and pull cats from anywhere in it.

By way of contrast, if there is no current, anglers generally seek out spots where cats ought to be nearby in every direction. The top of a hump that has cover along its slopes and good deep-water habitat all around it is an ideal location for still-water chumming.

With or without current, the best areas to chum also offer good holding areas for cats at a range of depths. Catfish will follow a chum line to find its source, but they generally won't stick around unless the habitat suits their tastes. Also cats seem to strongly favor specific depths on certain days. By chumming beside a drop or over a slope and close to stumps, rocks or deadfalls, anglers can get more cats to stack up in the areas they chum.

Long-term chumming works best for waters close to an angler's home simply because it's far more practical put out chum ahead of time and add more to it periodically. The chum attracts some catfish directly. More so, though, it is intended to attract and feed minnows, bream, and crawfish, as well as the really tiny critters that the bream and the crawfish eat. The catfish come to investigate the smell and find abundant food of many varieties. If chum remains in place for a week or two and the habitat in a spot is otherwise good, the number of cats using that area often will increase dramatically.

The long-term type of chumming is also great for bank-fishermen who have access only to a dock or to one or two areas along a lake's shore. By putting out chum the week before a bank-fishing outing, anglers often can draw numerous fish into a specific area that otherwise would have only scattered fish moving through it during a day.

Some commercially made chumming products are made specifically for long-term chumming. The blocks break up slowly, releasing scent and food as they do. Other good chumming material for the long-term approach includes fermented grain, cracked corn, and dog food. Big bags of off-brand, high-protein dog food provide a lot of food for catfish and many critters that catfish eat. And if dog food is broadcast over an area periodically, far more cats typically will begin using that area.

Of course, the very best way to chum an area, when circumstances allow, is to combine the short-term and long-term approaches. By keeping dog food or a chum block in an area for a couple of weeks, anglers can increase the number of cats using that particular area. Then, when they come to fish, they can put down some ground-up shad in a mesh bag to concentrate the cats beneath them.

Finally, waters downstream of grain-loading docks on rivers get "chummed" daily by spilled grain and are virtually always loaded with channel catfish. Likewise, waters immediately beside fish-cleaning docks at major marinas can be terrific in the evening. When fish heads and guts get tossed in a lake every afternoon, it doesn't take long for catfish to catch on.

In these types of areas, anglers who don't want to deal with chumming or who fish in places where chumming is prohibited can still enjoy the benefits of catfishing in chummed waters.

Traditional Methods

There's more than one way to catch a cat, and some very popular catfishing methods involve neither rods nor reels. Most "alternative" methods, as these are often dubbed in state regulations booklets, are actually far more traditional in the South than rod-and-reel fishing.

Jug-Fishing

Any time a jug starts dancing, things are about to get interesting. When a jug disappears, darting under like a crappie float, things are about to get downright exciting. Only heavyweight catfish yank most jugs completely under, and catching up with those fish and then getting them into the boat can be a pretty big adventure.

Running jugs is a fun and very effective way to catch catfish when the fish are in modest depths. It can be done in ponds, in coves of big reservoirs, or on any river that's big enough to float with the jugs in a boat.

Jug-fishing begins with several milk jugs, 2-liter drink bottles, or other plastic containers that can be sealed and could serve as big floats. Nylon cords are attached to each jug, with a hook and sometimes a weight added to each line. The line is then wrapped around the jug for neat storage until it's time to fish.

The basic jug-fishing technique is pretty elementary. Fishermen bait up a bunch of hooks on jug lines, toss the jugs out like a decoy spread, and wait for the jugs to start dancing or diving. In ponds or small lakes, jugs can be spread over a decent-sized area. In rivers, anglers generally keep their jugs fairly close together and drift downriver with them. "Spreads" of jugs are best kept tight on major reservoirs as well. It can be tough to keep track of widespread jugs on big water, especially if there is much other boating traffic.

Jugs can be run by day or by night. The daytime approach is clearly easier, but nighttime jug-fishing usually produces faster action. Nighttime jug-fishing is also extra fun, especially on ponds where no other boats are on the water. Keeping track of and chasing jugs by a spotlight beam can get pretty exciting.

Jug-fishermen usually use large landing nets to bring fish in the boat, making big sweeps to get fish and the jugs at the same time. If lines are set too deep for that, an alternative is to grab the jug and use it to retrieve the line. Experienced jug-fishermen know to never grab a line until they know for certain how large a catfish is pulling on the other end.

Circle hooks work well for jug lines because they hook fish effectively with no hookset. The best bait really depends on the waterway and the size and type of catfish anglers are going after. Cut shad or herring is a great bet in rivers for blue catfish. Chicken livers are tough to beat in good channel catfish waters.

Many anglers associate trotlining strictly with commercial catfishing, but fishermen throughout the South have for many years used small-scale trotlines to fish for fun and catch catfish to take home. A well-placed trotline often will catch just enough catfish in a night for a good Saturday afternoon fish fry. Whether they fish for food, fun, or catfish to sell, most trotliners place their lines in the evening, leave them to "fish" overnight, and take them up in the morning.

Trotlines are long, heavy-duty cords with any number of dropper lines spread along them, each with a baited hook on it. Trotlines can be 25 feet long or several hundred feet long, and can have any number of hooks on them. Running very long lines with high numbers often requires a commercial fishing license. Trotlines can be stretched across the bottom or through middle depths.

Trotlines can be purchased, pre-rigged, or made at home. Homemade lines offer a couple of major advantages. First, they are generally more durable than their pre-fab counterparts. Second, they can be made to anglers' specifications, based on where they

101

Traditional Methods

Figure 22. Trotlines, if well placed and baited with the right kind of offerings, provide good means for catching a nice mess of catfish.

will be run and the number, size, and style of hooks that anglers want to contend with.

The most challenging aspect of fishing trotlines for inexperienced anglers is spreading the line properly and bringing it up or checking it without creating a huge tangle. Two people make the process far easier.

The most exciting thing about running trotlines is the unknown element. Upon approaching a line in the morning, anglers never have any idea how many fish will be on it or just how big a catfish they may have caught.

Limblining

Limblines, as the name suggests, are lines that are tied to limbs. At the other end of each line is a baited hook. Some limblines also have weight added to them to keep live baits down in the strike zone. Others have a section of heavy intertube attached between the limb and the hook. The tube serves as a shock absorber, which spares broken line or straightened hooks when really large catfish latch on and have no place to go.

Limblines can be put out in all sorts of places and baited different ways for various catfish species. However, most serious sport limbline fishermen use them to capture big flatheads. They use live bullheads, gizzard shad, carp, or bream (where legal) and set the lines around shallow cover along the edges of big, deep holes. They leave the lines out through the night, which is when flatheads stray shallow to feed.

Limblines set up to target flatheads must be heavy duty. Most fishermen use nylon cord of 100- or 200-pound test and 10/O or larger saltwater-type circle hooks. Even with a piece of tube put in as a shock absorber, limblines should be tied to green, flexible limbs.

Yo-Yoing

Yo-yo rigs are essentially limblines; however, as the name suggests, each has a device called a "yo-yo" added to it. A small, spring-loaded reel that goes between the limb and the hook, a yo-yo is designed to go off when a fish tugs on the line, thus setting the hook. Yo-yos are especially nice for channel catfish, which are skilled at stealing bait from traditional limblines without getting hooked.

Beyond aiding in hooking cats, yo-yos offer several other advantages. First, they show which lines have been bit. If an angler wants to continue fishing traditional limblines after he gets fish from them, he must check every one to see whether any bait remains. Any yo-yo line that has been bit but doesn't have a cat on the end of it will be reeled up, with the hook hanging out of the waters. Additionally, yo-yo lines can easily be set to a big range of depths by just pulling out more or less line, and they can be stowed a lot more neatly between uses than loose limbline chords.

Handy as they are for catching a mess of modest-sized cats, yo-yos are not designed for heavyweight flatheads. Stout, short, and simple limblines are better suited for the task if anglers are baiting up with big live baits in flathead country.

Noodling

Some folks who don't want to wait for the catfish to find them instead go in after the fish—literally—wading along the edges of rivers and lakes and reaching into catfish-spawning cavities to wrestle out heavyweight fish.

Noodling, also commonly called grabbling, is highly efficient but it clearly is not for everyone. It's not uncommon for a noodler to get in a tug-of-war with a 50-pound-plus flathead catfish, with his arm as the rope and the cat biting down on his hand.

Different groups of noodlers use different specific techniques for finding and pulling out fish. Some use prods of some form to help locate fish, rocks to partially block cavity openings, or hooks and ropes to help get the cats out. The essence of the sport remains the same. All probe shoreline cavities, where cats hole up to spawn, yank the fish from their lairs, and then wrestle them into submission.

On scattered waterways throughout the South, folks work the same banks year after year and even generation after generation, usually in late spring or early summer. Some noodlers reach into natural cavities, under root clumps, between rocks, or along broken bluffs. Others maintain noodling "boxes," which are artificial nesting cavities that they plant just for the cats.

Whether or not cavities are natural, noodlers work along known spawning banks, moving from hole to hole. They typically use a boat to get from spot to spot, but they always get in the water before reaching into a cavity. One person reaches into each hole, and everyone else stands ready to help if needed. Occasionally noodlers grab (or get grabbed by) bigger and meaner cats than normal, and they need fast assistance to keep from getting dragged under.

All longtime noodlers have leather-tough hands and vivid stories about things like snapping turtles and extra-ornery flatheads. Some have scars that give credence to their tallest-seeming tales.

It's worth emphasizing that noodling is potentially dangerous. The cats, big and powerful, are in their element; the noodlers are not. Cuts, sprains, and broken bones all occur on occasion, and drowning is an undeniable possibility.

Check Regulations

Most methods other than rod-and-reel fishing have special regulations governing how, when, and where they can be done. Some methods are illegal in certain states. In other instances, a commercial license or other special permit is required. In most cases, regulations detail things like areas where trotlines cannot be run, the number of jugs permitted, or ways that lines must be labeled. Because regulations vary so much from state to state, it's essential that anglers check the rules before starting.

Chapter 5

Southern Hotspots

Altamaha River

The largest free-flowing river in Georgia, the Altamaha River also produces many of the Peach State's heftiest catfish. Beyond the state-record flathead catfish, the Altamaha has yielded numerous flatheads of even larger sizes to trotline and setline fishermen. A few of those cats have flirted with triple-digit weights. Additionally, the Altamaha produced Georgia's state-record channel catfish.

Georgia's state-record flathead, caught in 2000 by Gene Middleton, weighed 67 pounds, 8 ounces. The cat that Middleton's fish replaced in the books also came from the Altamaha, and biologists have shocked up and returned to the river numerous fish that would shatter the current record. The state-record channel catfish, pulled from the Altamaha in 1972 by Bobby Smithwick, weighed an impressive 44 pounds, 12 ounces.

More impressive than its top-end fish trophies, however, are the Altamaha's overall catfish densities and the scope of the cat-fishery. The river, which officially forms at the confluence of the Ocmulgee and Oconee Rivers, runs more than 135 miles to the Atlantic Ocean. It supports good numbers of high-quality flatheads and channels from the point where it forms (and well up both major headwaters, for that matter) almost to the open waters of the Atlantic Ocean. Through the river's tidal lower reaches, it also supports a very good population of white catfish.

Flatheads are not native to the Altamaha River. They showed in the Ocmulgee River during the late 1970s, probably having been transplanted from Georgia's Flint River, which they are not native to, either. More likely than not, some fishermen decided they liked the Flint's flatheads and wanted some of the big cats closer to home.

However they first arrived, by the late 1980s, flatheads had established themselves as the dominant catfish species in the Altamaha River by total numbers and weight, according to Rob Weller, fisheries biologist over the Altamaha for the Georgia Wildlife Resources Division (WRD). They also had spread downstream all the way to the river's tidal waters.

The flatheads apparently liked what they found in the Altamaha, which winds through hundreds of bends, many of which are littered with deadfalls. Age/growth work conducted by fisheries crews during the 1990s suggested that the flatheads were growing as fast as or faster than those in several other rivers and lakes where similar work had been done.

Densities and average weights increased steadily through the mid-1990s, when the population peaked, Weller said. Biologists would shock up more than 550 pounds of catfish hourly, as a riverwide average, when they did electro-fishing surveys. Through some stretches, hourly catch rates would exceed 1,000 pounds.

Since 1996, the total weights caught by electro-fishing have dropped off, largely due to increased fishing pressure, biologists believe. Catch rates have held fairly steady, but numbers of top-end fish have decreased, especially through the most accessible areas. Flatheads have gained tremendous popularity among hook-and-line anglers and setline fishermen alike, with both sets taking quite a few big fish home to eat.

As has been the case along many southeastern rivers where non-native flatheads have been introduced, the big cats have had a fair amount of controversy surrounding them almost from the onset. Voracious predators, the flatheads gobbled up native bullheads fairly quickly after becoming established. No one got too worked up about that, but when numbers of prized redbreast sunfish began to drop off, many longtime Altamaha River anglers became vocal. By the mid-1990s, redbreast numbers in the Altamaha had dropped close to 80 percent, Weller said.

With anti-flathead sentiment strong, the WRD invested a lot of time and effort seeking angler input through surveys and public meetings in hopes of determining the best course of action. Most anglers wanted to see flathead numbers reduced. They were strongly divided, however, regarding whether they would rather see that accomplished through increased angler harvest or some sort of removal program.

The WRD did establish an experimental removal zone within the upper Altamaha and the lower Ocmulgee, where they have shocked flatheads and removed them for several years. Numbers are down through that zone, and redbreast numbers are up. However, increased flathead fishing pressure and several years of drought conditions have made it difficult for biologists to determine how much of the population shift has been the direct result of the removal program.

Around the same time as they began the removal program, the WRD began to promote the flathead fishery more actively, educating anglers on how to find and catch the giant catfish. Through the 1990s, angler interest began to grow. By 2000, with a couple of state-record fish having been caught and numerous articles having been written about Altamaha River flatheads, interest had skyrocketed. The most recent creel surveys reveal that flatheads have become the No. 1 fish in the river, by the total weight of fish harvested, and they come in second only to largemouth bass in terms of angler effort.

While the flathead catch has declined some since its peak in 1996, Weller emphasized that there are still plenty of flatheads—including plenty of big flatheads—in the Altamaha River. Numbers of big fish are generally higher through the lower half of the river, but the next record flathead legitimately could come from anywhere along the river or from a tributary.

More than 25 boat ramps provide good access to the entire Altamaha River. Weller pointed toward Altamaha Fish Camp Landing, Jaycees Landing, Oglethorpe Bluff Landing, and Beards Bluff Landing as good starting points for flathead fishermen.

"Of course, what we always try to tell people is to go where other people don't go, which means getting away from access points. There are some fairly long stretches of river between some access points that don't get fished much." Weller said.

Anywhere along the river, dense cover, current breaks and a good range of depths are the keys to finding flatheads. More often than not, that combination is found along hard river bends, according to Weller. Outside bends form the deepest holes in the river, and eroding banks regularly topple shoreline trees into those holes. While sand-bluff banks often give away deep river holes, good electronics are invaluable for locating the deepest parts of holes, the locations of drops, downed trees inside holes, and, on occasion, catfish.

At times, flathead fishing can be very good along the historic channels of oxbows, which are scattered along the river. In fact, Gene Middleton caught his state record flathead from an oxbow known as Morgans Lake, not from the main channel of the river.

Through the river's lower reaches, where it spreads wider and begins splitting into marsh-bounded fingers, big holes become far less obvious. Anglers who understand the dynamics of tidal rivers and who know how to use their electronics to locate holes can find gold mines through this part of the river. Because the best spots are more difficult to find and often harder to set up over because of tides, they get less fishing pressure than big holes found farther up the river.

Palm-sized bluegills, shellcrackers, and redbreasts are the most popular bait species on the Altamaha. Georgia has no restrictions against using sunfish as bait, as long as they are caught legally, and limits for the sunfish are adhered to. Gizzard shad up to about a pound also make excellent bait for big Altamaha River flatheads. The state-record flathead bit a goldfish.

Because of complex and sometimes strong currents, anglers often anchor directly over the best areas on the Altamaha. If they can't set up over prime spots, many fishermen will anchor upstream and use big slip corks to suspend baits in the prime zone.

Weller suggests using at least 30-pound-test for Altamaha River flatheads, noting that some anglers go much heavier than that. Beyond the fact that flatheads grow to huge sizes, heavy cover absolutely abounds all along the river, and the biggest cats rarely stray far from the thickest stuff.

Weller noted that while flatheads attract most of the head-lines on the Altamaha, fishermen should not overlook the river's abundant channel cats. "Channel catfish are doing super," he said, noting they provide much faster action than flatheads typically do. Weller said that channels are plentiful throughout the Altamaha but that he typically sees the highest numbers of large fish down-stream of the town of Jesup.

Since channels use some of the same big river holes that flat-heads do, Weller suggested putting out lines for each species. Cut shad make outstanding channel catfish bait. Other good bets include frozen shrimp and chicken livers. Baits should be fished with enough weight to keep them on the bottom and cast downstream. Often, they won't stay there long. Through the river's far lower reaches, where marsh begins to replace forested banks, the same rigs and baits will produce mixed catches of channel and white catfish.

At the opposite end of the river and upstream from the Altamaha's official beginning, the river's two major tributaries, the Ocmulgee and Oconee Rivers, also offer good catfishing prospects. Creel surveys have shown channel catfish as the most caught species (of all fish, not just catfish) on the Ocmulgee River, both by total number and by total pounds. Fishing for channels is good just about anywhere on either river.

Both the Ocmulgee and the Oconee also support plenty of flatheads. However, since the lower Ocmulgee is part of the exper-imental flathead removal zone, the Oconee probably offers better big-cat prospects. The best flathead fishing on the Oconee is found downstream of the Interstate 16 crossing.

As a free-flowing river with a large watershed, the Altamaha's level and character vary quite a bit through the seasons. Fishing for most species is generally best when the river is well within its banks, not backed way up into surrounding swamps. Suitable river levels and good fishing usually begin around April and continue through late fall. Many anglers like midsummer best, but flathead fishing also can be outstanding during the fall.

"When the river is really high and muddy—that's when the big flat-heads get active," said Keith Sutton, author of *Fishing Arkansas* and *Catching Catfish*.

Sutton, known affectionately as "Catfish" by friends, has fished for cats from Canada to Brazil. However, with the catfish-rich waters of the Arkansas River flowing right through Little Rock, where Sutton lives, he never overlooks his "backyard cats."

The river was raging in May 1980 when a couple of fisher-men running snag lines in the Perry Lock and Dam tailwater cap-tured a flathead that weighed an incredible 139 pounds, 12 ounces. Reportedly the fish was one of several 50-pound-plus flat-heads they caught from the Arkansas River over the course of a few days.

Rod-and-reel sport fishermen haven't landed a triple-digit-weight flathead from the Arkansas River yet, but it may be just a matter of time. The state-record flathead, an 80-pound fish caught in 1989 by Whesley White, did come from the Arkansas River, and commercial anglers working the river have flirted with the century mark on numerous occasions.

Countless giant blue catfish also have come from the Arkansas River. The largest ever landed by a sport fisherman and officially weighed was an 86-pound, 15-ounce blue caught below Dardanelle Dam, and it was the state-record blue catfish at the time it was caught.

Sutton considers the Arkansas River one of the nation's pre-mier trophy catfish destinations, and he believes that it is largely overlooked. A lot of local fishermen—and plenty of commercial fishermen—know about the river's bounties, but it gets little acclaim outside Arkansas.

Rising in Colorado, high in the Rocky Mountains, the Arkan-sas River is 1,460 miles long, running the final 310 miles of its course through its namesake state. Only the Arkansas portion is in the South, and it offers the best catfishing along the river, anyway, according to Sutton.

"The Oklahoma part does have some pretty good catfishing, but nothing like what we have in Arkansas," he said.

From Fort Smith, where the river enters Arkansas, to its con-fluence with the Mighty Mississippi, the Arkansas River is impounded into a string of long, flowing pools by 12 separate dams. Sutton, who has fished the river hard for more than 20 years, has spent time on every single pool.

While there are hotspots scattered all along the river's flow, Sutton said that generally speaking the catfishing gets better and better the farther down the river one travels. In fact, his favorite stretch of the entire river is the 40-mile unimpounded section between the last dam on the river and the Mississippi River.

Just upstream of the last dam, officially named Wilbur Mill Dam but known almost universally as Dam No. 2, is a canal that connects the Arkansas and White Rivers. All barge traffic is diverted through the canal and the lower White River to the Mississippi.

The final run of the Arkansas is "wild and woolly," Sutton said, and looks much like the entire river certainly did a couple of hundred years ago. It winds through big bends with sandbars and deep holes that are absolutely full of trees. Those holes are full of big catfish, but they are difficult to fish.

The big-cat population through this part of the river undeni-ably benefits from its direct link to the Mississippi River, Sutton pointed out. "The Mississippi probably has more big catfish in it than any other river in the country, and a lot of Mississippi River fish move up into the Arkansas River at times."

All access to this stretch of river is from its ends. Anglers can put boats in either below Dam No. 2 or on the Mississippi. "To fish most of this section, you just about have spend a few days on the river," said Sutton, who annually takes a 4- or 5-day catfishing excur-sion on the lower Arkansas River.

That remoteness keeps crowds nonexistent, which is part of the appeal to Sutton. "I've been making trips there for 21 years, and some years I won't see anyone else downstream of the immediate tailwater. I never see more than a few other boats in a day."

The tailwater of Dam No. 2 is probably the best single spot on the entire river, Sutton said. During the spring, he has been to the Dam No. 2 tailwater and seen almost everyone who was fishing catching numerous 20-pound-plus flathead catfish.

Whether at Dam No. 2 or Fort Smith Dam, at the opposite end of the state, tailwaters provide the best overall opportunity for catfishermen along the Arkansas River, according to Sutton. Catfish of all three species pile up in the tailwaters, and currents cause the fish to feed actively.

One of the best things about tailwaters below the dams along the Arkansas River is that every one has good shoreline access. Sutton noted. In fact, bank-fishermen can get much closer to the dams than boating anglers can. Closed zones for boaters extend 100 yards below the dams. Because the best fishing is often quite close to dams, boating anglers often go as far upstream as they are permitted to and make long casts toward the dam with surf-casting rods.

Many shoreline anglers also use surf-casting gear because the best currents are often well away from the bank. They make long casts angled across the river and upstream, and then let their offerings tumble downstream across the bottom. They use several ounces of weight, both for the sake of making long casts and for getting baits down to the catfish in the strong currents.

Almost all tailwater fishermen use two-hook rigs, Sutton said. The basic rig is a modified three-way rig, tied with two leaders off one of the eyes of a three-way swivel or with an extra dropper tied to a loop knot up the main line, up from the three-way swivel. Weights commonly used range from 4 to 8 ounces, depending on the amount of water running. Common hook sizes range from 4/O to 6/O.

Snags are frequent, Sutton conceded. "You're gonna lose a bunch of tackle, especially weights. However, you have to get down to the bottom, in the current and around the rocks, to catch catfish."

In addition to the tailwaters, hundreds of wing dams create outstanding habitat for catfish throughout the river. Most wing dams are concentrated in the upper ends of the pools, within the first several miles downstream of each dam. Some are located farther down pools, however.

Wing dams, or wing dikes, as they are also known, are rock jetties built perpendicular to the river channel. They are designed to funnel the river's flow, which lessens sedimentation within the river channel and reduces the need for dredging.

The end result is a rocky structure with current pushing across it, deep scour holes immediately upstream and downstream of the wing dam, eddies, and circling currents. The placement of the holes and the nature of the currents vary from wing dam to wing dam and from day to day, according to the dam's specific configuration and the amount of water being poured through the upstream hydroelectric dam.

All offer good cover for cats, according to Sutton, and by doing a bit of searching with electronics and trying out various positions along wing dams, fishermen can usually find plenty of cats. Generally speaking, Sutton likes to set up almost straight off the end of a wing dam and fish the head of the big scour hole that begins right where the rocks taper off.

Along with tailwater offerings and wing dams, all the river's pools offer great catfish habitat in and around many classic river holes that form along major outside bends. Big bends, often fronted by bluffs, offer a big range of depths in a single area, and most are cluttered with trees that have fallen into them, giving catfish great cover to relate to.

Dardanelle Pool, between Fort Smith and Little Rock, also has a literal hotspot on it, Sutton pointed out. A nuclear power plant uses river water for cooling operations, and warm water gets discharged back into the river. The warm water holds big concentrations of baitfish and catfish year 'round, and gets especially good through the middle of winter.

Large and more lake-like than most other Arkansas River pools, Dardanelle also offers a lot of good habitat around inundated creek and river channels, Sutton pointed out. "There are a lot of ledges and holes with timber and brush down in them—a lot of what I think of as really good flathead habitat," he said.

Flathead fishermen look for distinctive features along creek and river channels that are tangled with some type of woody cover. They gear up heavy and fish mostly with live bluegills or gizzard shad. Most do all their serious fishing at night, when the big flatheads are most active.

Blue catfish, while abundant throughout the Arkansas portion of the Arkansas River, don't get much targeted pressure on the river. "There are plenty of them in there," Sutton said. "In fact, I'd say that every pool on the river has the potential to produce 50-pound-plus blues any given day. There just aren't many people doing what I would consider serious fishing for blue catfish."

Serious fishing for blue cats begins with baiting up for them, Sutton said. He pointed toward big chunks of cut shad or herring as the only real choice for anglers who want to target trophy blues, and the first few miles downstream of each dam as the best blue cat waters. The best time, he said, is during the spring when the river is running at 25,000 to 50,000 cubic feet per second.

Sutton said that fishermen who simply want fast catfishing action or fish to take home can find plenty of channel catfish pretty much anywhere along the river. "You can catch channel catfish up to about 5 pounds all day long," he said. "The river is just alive with them."

In terms of seasons, Sutton said that late spring probably offers the biggest catches of heavyweight fish, overall. The fish move upstream to spawn and get piled up beneath dams, and typically high flows make for active cats.

Sutton emphasized, however, that the Arkansas River undeniably is a year-round catfishing river. Fishing can be outstanding in the river even through midwinter, he has found, and, best of all, "You'll have it all to your self!"

Cape Fear River

Seven.

That's the number of flathead catfish that biologists stocked in the Cape Fear River in the mid-1960s. It's probably safe to say that at that time no one had any idea what kind of fishery would develop from that single small stocking.

North Carolina's classic big-cat fishery, the Cape Fear River offers more than 100 miles of picture-perfect catfish habitat as it twists through the coastal plain. The biggest flathead and blue catfish on record from North Carolina came from the Cape Fear, as did the fish that both of those replaced in the record books. Over the years, the river's dark waters have produced hundreds of enormous flatheads and blues.

The state-record flathead, which weighed 69 pounds, was caught by Ed Davis in 1994. The state-record blue catfish, which tipped the scales to 80 pounds, was caught in 1999 by Keith Davis (unrelated to Ed Davis).

Ed Davis, who at one time held the state record for flathead and blue catfish, both from the Cape Fear River, also has his name written all over the National Fresh Water Fishing Hall of Fame record book. Davis holds 15 line-class world records for catfish, all from the Cape Fear and its tributaries, and some under the Fly-Fishing classification. Among Davis' records are a 47-pound blue that he caught on 4-pound-test line and a 52-pound flathead that he caught on 2-pound-test!

No name is more closely associated with Cape Fear catfish than that of Ed Davis, and no other fisherman knows the river better. While Davis' health no longer permits him to fish, no one has ever been more dedicated to Cape Fear catfishing. A normal Ed Davis fishing trip was 72 hours long, with every minute spent on the river, scouting by day and fishing by night.

Most folks who know much about fishing for big cats on the Cape Fear learned it from Davis—or they learned from someone who learned from Davis. They point to him as the one who taught them about catfishing and catfish conservation.

As is the case on many big-cat waterways, trotline and setline fishermen have caught blues and flatheads that would break the state record on several occasions. Many veteran hook-and-line anglers, meanwhile, contend they have had a record fish hooked at least once, and most believe that numerous record-breakers remain in the river.

The Cape Fear's dark waters actually support a great population of channel catfish, including some really big ones. Because of the river's abundant jumbo-sized flatheads and blues, however, the channel cats tend to get overlooked. Big blues outnumber big flatheads in the river, according to Davis, but there are plenty of both to keep catfishermen happy.

From its origin below the dam at Lake Jordan, the Cape Fear River twists through deep bend after deep bend all the way to the coast, alternating between shallow stretches and deep holes and trading sandy and rocky bottoms. Most hard riverbends have deep

Figure 23. Along with the North Carolina state-record flathead, which weighed 69 pounds, Ed Davis holds numerous line-class world records. Photo courtesy of Ed Davis.

water associated with them and tangles of downed timber within them, providing wonderful hideouts for big catfish.

Of course, every time a big tropical weather system spins over the North Carolina coast, which seems to happen about every other year, hundreds of new trees get washed or blown into the river. Flood conditions, whether they come from spring rains or hurricanes, repeatedly rearrange the river's holes, channels, and sandbars.

The Cape Fear is extremely fertile, supporting thriving populations of bream, small catfish, and assorted other species that provide food for the big cats throughout the year. Stomach content surveys done with large Cape Fear flatheads revealed that the big cats are especially fond of other catfish for dinner.

In addition to the year-'round food sources, several species of herring and shad, and even eels move up the Cape Fear seasonally, supplementing the forage base. Live eels, when available, are favored baits of Cape Fear anglers for big flatheads. Big pieces of cut eel also account for a lot of blues.

Because of the diversity of food sources, Davis suggested "setting the table" with several types of bait. "Steak might be your favorite food," he said, "but after a few days of eating it three times a day, you would get tired of that steak." Davis pointed toward live and cut eels, venison heart, gizzard shad, carp, and assorted sunfish as potentially good baits for flatheads and blues.

Anglers catch big Cape Fear catfish from as far up the river as they are able to navigate all the way to tidal reaches. Some anglers consider the waters between Fayetteville and Lock 3, which is the uppermost of three locks on the river, as the river's prime zone. This section yielded the last two state-record flatheads, according to Keith Ashley, a fisheries biologist for the North Carolina Wildlife Resources Commission, who spends a lot of work time on the Cape Fear.

A public ramp accesses this stretch of the river at Arnett Park, off state Highway 87, south of Fayetteville. Fishermen should look for classic river holes on outside bends, with deep water close to shallow water, plenty of fallen trees in and around the holes, and good current breaks.

"The Cape Fear has so much fine habitat, with its bends and curves and bottom shrubbery, that if someone wants to look, they can find a good spot just about anywhere along the river," according to Davis.

Davis and another longtime Cape Fear catfisherman, Wayne Champion, once spent an entire week exploring the river from the third lock almost to the mouth of the river. They caught a lot of catfish in places they had never even laid eyes on before, Davis said.

Davis pointed toward deep holes as the areas to concentrate on, but he stressed that the fish won't necessarily be in the bottom of the hole. The best action often occurs on the shallow flat along the inside bend, especially on summer nights, he pointed out. Davis noted that on moonlit nights, the dark side of the river is best.

For Cape Fear blues, big pieces of cut shad or eel can simply be laid out on the bottom, usually along the edges of holes. For flatheads, live baits generally need to be suspended off the bottom, and fishermen use a lot of innovative rigs to suspend baits where they want them.

The river's often-strong currents, irregular bottom, and tangles of timber make it impractical to impossible to anchor over the fish in many instances. Davis pointed toward slip floats that are big enough to suspend several ounces of weight, side-planers, and jugs set up with release clips as all being valuable tools for fishing the Cape Fear effectively.

No easily identifiable rig or setup is a catch-all answer on the Cape Fear, he stressed. Every hole along the river is configured differently, and different seasons and water levels make any given hole quite different to fish from one trip to another. Generally speaking, it takes 3 or 4 ounces of weight to hold baits in place on the Cape Fear, according to Davis. He pointed toward 7/O Kahle hooks as being well suited for most baits he would use for big Cape Fear cats.

Beyond the main branch of the Cape Fear, the Northeast Cape Fear produces more than its share of jumbo-sized catfish, as does the lower end of the Black River, another major tributary. Both streams are similar in character to the main river, and flatheads hold in the same types of holes.

Another big-cat gem in the Cape Fear system—particularly for jumbo flatheads—is Lake Sutton, a 1,000-acre cooling pond for a coal-burning plant on a Cape Fear tributary. Flatheads found their way into Lake Sutton some time in the late 1980s or early 1990s and have thrived in its fertile waters.

Biologists experimented with shocking flatheads to remove them from the lake in the early 1990s because of the big fish's likely impact on bass and bream populations. Such efforts were quickly abandoned, though, as it soon became obvious that the fish were very well established. Flathead specialists have since embraced the fishery and target Lake Sutton's big fish quite seriously.

Lake Sutton is actually divided by internal dikes into a series of "ponds." The dikes and channels create good structure for the flatheads and make their locations very predictable. Ashley pointed toward Lake No. 3 as a good spot to look for big flatheads because of an old creek channel that cuts through it. He said that any deep holes and channels in the ponds are likely areas for finding fish.

Because Lake Sutton is used for cooling operations, it stays warm through the winter and is a literal flathead hotspot through the cool months. It's not strictly a cold-weather catfishing hole, though. Anglers who head out on Lake Sutton on summer nights sometimes hook up with mammoth flatheads.

The entire Cape Fear River system is definitely a four-season fishery. The first time I spoke to Ed Davis was during December, and he had just returned from a trip to the river. He and a couple of friends had caught and released 63 catfish in a few days, including several in the 50-pound range.

Cumberland River

"I've had the world-record flathead on my line in this river," Donny Hall told me, as he began cutting up skipjack to lay out lines for Cumberland River catfish.

Hall, a guide from Nashville, admits he can't confirm his assertion. He never saw the fish. Nevertheless, he does not hesitate in stating that it was a record cat. Hall has caught dozens of 50-pound-plus catfish (some way over 50), and this fish was in a class by itself. He had it on for a long time and never even felt like he gained ground.

Hall has beefed up his tackle since that day, which was several years ago. He uses powerful custom catfish rods of his own design and 130-pound-test braided line, and he has no doubt that he is equipped to land the next record fish that takes one of his baits.

The Cumberland River's record-cat potential was proven in 1998 when it produced Tennessee's state-record blue catfish. Robert E. Lewis caught the super-sized blue, which weighed in at an even 112 pounds. While never submitted for world-record consideration, it bested the fish that held the top spot at the time and falls less than five pounds shy of the current world record.

Donny Hall has fished the Cumberland River since he was a kid. He grew up along the river, just outside Nashville, and he would fish the Cumberland from its banks before he had a boat. His guide service is called Old Hickory Lake Guide Service, but he actually runs trips on more than 150 miles of the Cumberland. He also guides quite a bit for catfish on the Tennessee River.

The Cumberland River rises in the mountains of Kentucky, dips through Tennessee for much of its course, and then completes its run back in Kentucky, where it adds its flow to the Ohio River. A major river, but not a huge river, the Cumberland is large enough to be navigable by barges from Nashville downstream to its mouth.

Five major impoundments—Cumberland, Cordell Hull, Old Hickory, Cheatham, and Barkley—contain most of the Cumberland's length.

All offer good catfishing, as does the river above Cumberland Lake. The final two impoundments in the system, Cheatham and Barkley, are best known for producing heavyweight flatheads and blues; Old Hickory to a lesser extent. From the headwaters to Cordell Hull dam, channel cats dominate the catfish catch.

The lower half of the Cumberland River system, along with being more the size river that jumbo blues and flatheads favor, offers an absolute abundance of food for cats of all sizes. Crawfish abound on rocky banks, various sunfish cruise all types of banks, and threadfin and gizzard shad and skipjack herring all form big schools in the river's open waters.

Habitat is likewise diverse and very good. The river winds through countless bluff-lined bends, which have deep holes beside them. Across from the bluffs, shallower mud banks often have downed trees along them. Meanwhile, remnants of several old lock-and-dam structures provide additional habitat. Some have walls intact. Others are essentially piles of rubble. All provide good holding areas for catfish.

The upper end of Barkley Lake, which produced the Tennessee state-record blue catfish, is nationally famous for its super-sized cats. Probably the best-known single spot through this stretch is the

Cumberland Steam Plant, which has a warm-water discharge that congregates baitfish and catfish alike through the winter.

This section easily gets the most catfishing pressure, however, by commercial and recreational anglers, and many anglers, including Hall, believe the fishery has been impacted. Barkley is big, though, spreading over 57,200 acres, and it undoubtedly still has plenty of jumbo cats in it.

Lake Barkley's tailwater, 20 miles or so from the mouth of the Cumberland, is famous in Kentucky for the big catfish it produces. Blues easily dominate the catfish catch in the Barkley tailwater, but it also yields some jumbo flatheads. Channel cats are well represented, but most tailwater catfishermen fish with large enough chunks of cut skipjack or gizzard shad to limit their channel cat catch.

Shoreline access is possible beside the tailwater, but most serious catfishermen use boats. Swift currents and a very rocky bottom pretty much dictate vertical presentations for getting baits down to cats but avoiding staying snagged. Most fishermen work fairly close to the dam, bouncing cut bait off the bottom with three-way rigs. Fishing is best when some turbines are on and others are off.

Hall does most of his serious Cumberland River catfishing on Cheatham Lake, which impounds the section of river that winds through downtown Nashville. Cheatham is 68 miles long, impounds a little less than 7,500 acres and is very riverine in character. At various times, Hall fishes section of the river from Old Hickory Dam all the way to Cheatham Dam.

During the spring, Hall concentrates most of his efforts on the middle section of the lake, as a lot of catfish tend to be moving from deep holes throughout the lake's lower half toward the Old Hickory tailwater. Channel catfish, which dominate Hall's catch that time of year, commonly serve up fast action.

Hall also spends a fair number of spring days on Old Hickory, which has an outstanding channel catfish population. Cheatham is operated as a flood-control lake, and after heavy spring rains it can turn high and muddy in a hurry. Old Hickory spreads into a much broader basin than its downstream neighbor, and its level is held pretty constant because of heavy shoreline development. Therefore, when Cheatham is rocking, fishing conditions on Old Hickory typically remain good

On either lake, Hall baits several bottom rigs with small pieces of skipjack or gizzard shad and spreads them around the boat. He pointed toward waters in the 10- to 20-foot depth range at the tops of ledges, especially near the mouths of creeks, as good areas to set up.

As spring progresses, Hall will spend more time fishing close to Old Hickory Dam. All three species spawn around abundant rocky cover in the tailwater portion, and he does well before and after the spawn. Cats can be caught in shallow water up and down the river during late spring and early summer, Hall said, but he catches better-quality fish up the river.

Catfish get tough to catch during the spawn, but with three species of fish and an abundance of each, there are plenty of cats in pre- and post-spawn modes even during the peak of the spawn, which Hall said usually occurs around Memorial Day.

As summer sets in, Hall moves up even farther, and he concentrates most of his dog-days' efforts on the waters immediately below the dam. Hall sets up in eddy areas, ideally beside currents created by turbines that are running, and drifts with big chunks of skipjack fished on tight lines straight below him. Fishing is best in the tailwater when two or three of Old Hickory's four generators are running, Hall has found.

Once summer gives way to fall, Hall begins moving back down river, where big cats begin orienting to big holes. He pointed toward the area around Neelys Bend, which sets just east of Nashville as a good area to begin looking for fish. He keys on big holes, but looks for mud banks instead of rock banks. He will anchor pretty close to shore and put a couple of lines almost on the bank and spread others farther out into the deep water.

As fall gives way to winter, Hall continues to work his way down the lake. He does most of his winter fishing in ten miles or so of river between Glower Island and Ashland City. "In that area, there are probably 300 to 400 good holes," Hall said. "Any sharp ledge is apt to have catfish below it during the winter."

Hall noted that the catfish really congregate in big schools during winter. "If you catch a couple right away, you're probably getting ready to load the boat," he said.

Hall catches some heavyweight channels in the winter, along with blues and flatheads of all sizes. He fishes mostly with cut skipjack or shad, sometimes putting down one or two big live shad for flatheads. If an angler specifically wants to catch flatheads, Hall will put down all live bait.

When Hall puts big pieces of bait down in big-cat waters, he leaves nothing to chance. He uses Donny Hall Custom Catfish Rods, which are heavy-duty S-Glass rods with saltwater-type blanks. He matches his rods with Abu Garcia 7000 reels, spooled with 130-pound-test SpiderWire.

Hall does most of his fishing with a basic Carolina rig, putting a barrel weight on the main line and then adding a heavy swivel and a couple feet of leader. Weights range from 1 to 8 ounces, depending on depths and strength of currents. His hook of choice for big-cat applications is a 10/O Gamakatsu hook.

If he doesn't expect super-sized cats in the mix, Hall will downsize everything a bit, with rigs that center around heavy flippin' sticks. "Those are good for smaller fish—up to about 50 pounds," he said. "Bigger than that, you're likely to break a rod."

Hall stated concern about the impact of commercial fishing on the Cumberland River. "Through the upper part of Barkley, you can't go a quarter-mile without seeing a trotline. You can about wipe out a whole section of river with that much pressure," he said.

Through the urging of Hall and other concerned sport fishermen, Tennessee Wildlife Resources Agency has initiated a research project to look more closely than they previously have at the commercial fishing harvest and its potential impact.

Hall hopes that, after the results of that study have been examined, tighter restrictions might be put on commercial fishing. Hall, who releases all the big cats he catches, wants to see the Cumberland stay as good as it is—and as it has been since he was a boy, fishing from the banks around Nashville.

James and Rappahannock Rivers

Virginia's James and Rappahannock Rivers have a lot in common. Both rise in the mountains, where tumbling trout-filled creeks join forces, and then gain size over many miles as cool, clear smallmouth rivers before tumbling over the Fall Line to the Atlantic coastal plain. Both are heavily influenced by tides through their lower reaches, and both terminate in Chesapeake Bay. Most importantly to catfishermen, both are world-class destinations for bruiser blue catfish throughout their tidal portions.

In many ways, however, the two rivers are vastly different. Virginia's largest river, the James is a massive flow. Its valley is fairly flat, heavily developed, and largely industrialized. The Rappahannock, on the other hand, cuts a relatively narrow course, winding among abundant sandy bluffs through landscapes that look little different than they would have 100 years ago.

Boat channels, dredging operations, bridge pilings, and commercial docks create some of the best holes on the James. Other holes lie hundreds of yards from the bank and can be located only through good map- and graph-reading skills. On the Rappahannock, most of the best spots to fish for big blues are large classic river holes, which form along bends in the river, downstream of islands and in mouths of tributaries.

Both rivers sprang into prominence as catfish destinations in the late 1980s and early 1990s. Non-native blue catfish, which had been introduced into the rivers in the late 1970s, had quietly grown large in the two rivers. Serious sport catfishing was not popular in Virginia, and few people fished for or even knew about the fish for several years. Then, seemingly out of nowhere, anglers started bringing in fish that weighed 30 pounds or more. Word of the cats spread quickly, and serious catfishing caught on.

The popularity of sport catfishing has increased ever since on Virginia's tidal waters. The blue catfish state record has been broken several times over the years, with both rivers and one tributary having taken turns with the record. The state record currently stands at 71 pounds, 12 ounces, with a fish caught from the Dutch Gap area of the James River in 1999. Veterans of these two rivers believe there are still bigger cats waiting to be caught.

The Rappahannock River has a little less than 20 miles of tidal waters, beginning at Fredericksburg, which straddles the Fall Line. The James' tidal waters, which begin immediately downstream of Richmond, extend about 50 miles downstream before opening into the bay.

Figure 24. Virginia's James and Rappahannock rivers, both major tidal rivers, have the common denominator of supporting world-class blue catfish fisheries.

Shocking surveys conducted by the Virginia Department of Game and Inland Fisheries (VDGIF) suggest that the best fishing for blues on the Rappahannock begins a few miles downstream of Fredricksburg and extends approximately to Leedstown. Prime waters for big blues on the James begin right at the Fall Line and continue roughly to the Surry Nuclear Plant.

The James and Rappahannock Rivers both support outstanding blue catfish populations, but the James is clearly the state's top river, in terms of the sheer number of trophy cats it yields. That is easily seen by glancing at a single year's results from an angler recognition program operated by the VDGIF.

Anglers earn awards, called citations, for catching fish that exceed predetermined "trophy" sizes for various popular species. Blue catfish must weigh at least 20 pounds to earn a citation or be at least 34 inches long, if released. In 2000, of 1,384 blue catfish citations awarded, 1,000 were for James River cats. When the James and Rappahannock fisheries were developing and both received only modest use, the two rivers would trade turns as top citation cat producers. Over time, though, the James emerged as the clear No. 1 big-cat river.

When talking about Virginia's tidal-water catfish, it would be neglectful to fail to look also at two of the James' largest tributaries, the Chickahominy and Appomattox Rivers. Blue and channel catfish abound in both rivers, providing anglers with many more miles of catfish waters to explore.

The Appomattox produced a 66-pound, 8-ounce blue in the 1990s that stood for a few years as the state record. The Chickahominy ranked second only to the James in blue catfish citations in 2000 with 112 30-pound-plus cats registered. It nosed out the Rappahannock, which normally holds the No. 2 spot, by two trophy catfish.

Neither the Chickahominy nor the Appomattox produces nearly as many 40-pound-class catfish as do the big rivers they feed, but blues up to about 25 pounds absolutely abound in both tributaries.

Throughout Virginia's tidal blue catfish waters, anglers focus on fairly deep water throughout the year. They look for deep holes that have shallow water nearby and cover within them. Most anglers also like to see forage and catfish on their graphs before they set up.

Finding current is essential for finding active cats, and fish relate differently to spots according to the direction and strength of the current. Being tidally influenced for many miles, these waters vary dramatically in character according to the stage and strength of the tide, the amount of water flowing down the river and the specific spot along the river. Tidal fishing is a complex equation, and veteran anglers on these rivers have learned favorite spots for a host of conditions.

Stomach-content surveys conducted by VDGIF biologists on blue catfish from tidal rivers provide good insights that should be beneficial to fishermen. Prevalent forage varied significantly by size of catfish and by season. Catfish of less than about 20 inches long fed on a wide variety of things, including crawfish, assorted mollusks, aquatic insects, and small baitfish. Larger blues fed almost exclusively on fish.

White perch were the most important species in the diet of the larger blues through spring, followed by minnows, threadfin and gizzard shad, and anadromous shad and herring species. During summer, white perch were tops, by far, followed by young-of the-year anadromous shad and herring, gizzard and threadfin shad, and catfish. In the fall, young-of-the-year anadromous shad and herring took over as the most important forage for big blues, followed by gizzard and threadfin shad, eels, and catfish.

Almost all anglers who target big blues fish with whole or cut fish. Gizzard shad, cut into big strips, probably are the most popular bait. However, some anglers do favor the white perch, just as the catfish do through much of the year, and young anadromous shad and herring make great fall bait if anglers are able to find and net some. Live and cut eels are also very popular during summer and early fall and are even available in some bait stores.

Most anglers focus on deep holes, whether natural or man-made, but put baits both in the deep waters and the shallow water near them. They typically spread out several baits, using Carolina rigs or three-way rigs weighted with 2 to 4 ounces of lead to get all the rigs to the bottom.

While blues are clearly the spotlight species in the Virginia sport catfishing picture, the James also supports a very good and still developing flathead fishery. Some flatheads roam the tidal portion of the river, but numbers are highest from Richmond upstream to the river's headwaters.

Upstream of Richmond, where the James River tumbles over rocky shoals from the piedmont to the coastal plain, the river is best known for its fine canoeing and smallmouth bass fishing. Big bluff holes throughout the upper river hold heavyweight flatheads, how-ever, and these bruisers don't get much attention from fishermen.

Flathead fishing is also excellent right through Richmond. Deep rocky holes throughout the downtown section hold a lot of big flatheads. Remnants of historic dams and bridges, along with the river's natural drop along the Fall Line, create deep, slack holes beside swifter water, which makes for ideal flathead habitat.

In 2000, the James produced 43 citation-earning flatheads, making it the state's No. 2 producer. It also produced Virginia's largest flathead in the same year. Flatheads haven't been in the James as long as blues have, and shocking surveys reveal that numbers are increas-ing in the tidal portion of the river.

No one knows at this point how prevalent flatheads will become or how large they will grow on the James. Based on what has happened along much of the Atlantic Coast, however, they are likely to expand heavily through the river's tidal waters and grow to heavyweight proportions, side by side with the big blues.

Meanwhile, channel catfish abound throughout the James River system and in the Rappahannock. The Rappahannock, in fact, produced Virginia's state record channel catfish. Caught by Sue Stanley in 1992, the jumbo catfish weighed in at 31 pounds, 8 ounces.

Anglers looking for fast action, more so than giant fish, can usually find plenty of channel catfish up to about 5 or 6 pounds on any of the tidal rivers. The channels use a lot of the same types of holes as the blues do, and they bite well year 'round. The biggest difference, from a strategy standpoint, is that anglers targeting channel catfish should rig up with chicken livers, dip bait, or small pieces of cut shad, instead of big chunks of cut bait. Catches actually will typically include a pretty good mix of channels and blues, but blues caught on those types of bait will generally weigh 10 pounds or less.

Through the lower reaches of the James and the Rappahannock and in tidal creeks along both rivers, white catfish also abound. The white cats, which don't grow very large, extend even into the brackish water.

The combined daily limit for flathead, blue, channel, and white catfish and bullheads in Virginia is 20 fish. However, downstream of the Fall Line, anglers may keep unlimited numbers of catfish. That recognized, fishermen who target big blues in the tidal portions of the James River system and the Rappahannock have as strong a release ethic as virtually any group of catfishermen.

Lake Texoma

The big-cat tradition runs deep on Lake Texoma, a massive reservoir along the Texas/Oklahoma border. In the 1970s, long before serious sport-fishing for jumbo catfish had gained popularity through most of the country, fishermen were traveling long distances to target the giant blue catfish that would (and still do) congregate through the lower end of Lake Texoma during winter and early spring.

Channel, flathead, and blue catfish are all native to the Red River, which Texoma impounds. All three species are well represented and grow to big sizes, but heavyweight blues are the lake's signature. Texoma has produced four line-class world-record blue catfish, as listed in *Official World and USA State Fresh Water Angling Records* (2002).

The biggest cat ever weighed from the lake, a trotline fish, weighed 116 pounds, and is the biggest catfish on record from anywhere in Texas. The Texas state record rod-and-reel blue also came from Texoma. Reyez Martinez caught the heavyweight blue, which weighed an even 100 pounds, in March 2000.

Texoma has all the right ingredients for producing huge blues, according to Bruce Hysmith, district fisheries supervisor of the Lake Texoma fisheries office of the Texas Department of Parks and Wildlife.

"For starters, blue catfish are big-water fish, and Lake Texoma definitely is big water at 89,000 acres," Hysmith said. "It also pulls nutrients from a big watershed of 45,000 square miles."

Hysmith also pointed toward chloride, which is deposited in soils through portions of the watershed and therefore gets infused into the lake with every good rain, as benefiting the lake's productivity. "The catfish benefit from that salt in the system," he said, noting that the chloride helps account for the lake remaining so productive, despite having been built in the 1940s.

Fishermen discovered during the 1970s the big blue catfish that congregate in the lower lake each winter. Striper fishermen would see big marks on their graphs, down pretty deep, that looked like umbrellas on the paper. Experimentation revealed that the umbrellas were huge blue catfish, and the fishermen soon began to figure out how to catch them.

Word spread quickly, not surprisingly, when fishermen started pulling up big catches of 30-, 40-, and 50-pound fish. A local guide's wife caught a real giant that got a lot of publicity, and that really blew the lid off the whole thing, Hysmith recalled.

Prime time for giant blues on Lake Texoma is from December through March, according to Hysmith. During that time almost all of Texoma's big blues concentrate in the lake's lower main body.

They cruise the deep waters of the Red River channel, primarily between the confluence of the Red and Washita Rivers and the dam.

Fishermen ride both sides of the old river channel, looking for big marks in 50 to 55 feet of water. Most anglers begin searching along the edge of a big flat called "the Tabletop," which sets inside a big bend in the river channel and is about 40 feet deep. "Smaller fish will be on the tabletop," Hysmith said. "The big blues will be down in the channel beside it."

Beginning near the Tabletop and working toward the dam, fishermen will hunt "umbrellas," which may not be right on the bottom but usually will be in the lower two-thirds of the water column. When they locate fish, which rarely are loners, they kill the outboard and count baits down to the appropriate depth (or drop them all the way down if the fish are on or very near the bottom). With lines down, they drift and wait for the show to begin.

"Of course, the more you pick up on the graph, the better your chances," Hysmith said.

Texoma blues stay fat and happy on abundant threadfin and gizzard shad. However, gizzard shad are clearly the baitfish of choice for most anglers who target trophy blues, Hysmith said. He pointed out that beyond growing larger than threadfins, gizzard shad are very oily.

"When a fish bites, that oil really disperses, and that often triggers more bites," he said.

Most fishermen use big strips of cut shad (or even whole, dead shad) fished on Carolina rigs with just enough weight to hold the lines straight down. The fish aren't line-shy in the depths of Lake Texoma, so most fishermen gear up heavily. Knowing any fish that bites could be the next world record, they use heavy monofilament or braid, rods that have a lot of backbone, and geared-down baitcasting reels.

While blue catfish are somewhat famous for their screaming initial runs, Hysmith noted that quite often a fish hooked in the deep water will come up with little resistance at first, almost like it is oblivious to being hooked. "Until he sees the boat, that is. Then he'll go absolutely crazy!" Hysmith said.

Late winter and early spring also attract a lot of jug-fishermen to Lake Texoma. Channel cats of all sizes and small to medium-sized blues cruise flats and create sometimes-fabulous action to anglers who run jugs, usually baited with livers, shrimp, or cut shad.

"People come from all over to jug-fish for catfish that time of year," he said. "Entire families come for a week at a time, year after year."

As spring progresses, the big blue catfish begin working their way up Texoma's two big river arms—a progression that will continue into the summer. The biggest blues rarely stray far from the main river channels, but they will travel far upriver from the deep main body of the lake. By the time spring has given way to summer, the big blues typically have worked their way well up the rivers, even into moving waters.

Biologists from both Texas and Oklahoma have shocked up some tremendously big blue catfish far up the river arms during spring and summer, Hysmith noted, and the lake-record blue came from well up the Red River that time of year. Historically, trotliners have far outnumbered rod-and-reel anglers up the rivers. Over the past several years, however, sport rod-and-reel fishermen have begun figuring out the spring/summer patterns.

The blues pile up along river bends, where a big range of depths can be found in close proximity. They often hold in the deepest water through the day, during which time they can be somewhat difficult to catch. At night, they move shallow and feed well. Unlike the deep-holding winter cats, these blues take off like Indy cars as soon as they grab a bait.

About the time the blue catfish start up the rivers, the flatheads generally become more active. Far less numerous than blues and channels, flatheads get very little targeted fishing pressure by Lake Texoma fishermen. Folks who do target them look for bends in the old creek and river channels that cut close to cover-rich banks and dangle live bait. Most dangle those offerings on limblines or trotlines.

Late in the spring and on into summer, a unique brand of catfisherman converges on Lake Texoma each year. Anglers use float tubes to work quietly along rocky banks and present live crawfish to abundant channel cats, which cruise the rocky banks before and after the spawn.

The channel cats move up the creeks early in the year because spring rains warm their waters quickly. The same rains also dislodge a lot of food from along the shore. Catfish like the rocky banks partly because they like the protein-rich crawfish that abound along rocky shores. Plus, they often spawn in crevices between the rocks, generally in June.

Two or three anglers will go out together in a pontoon, each with his float tube aboard, Hysmith explained. They will pick a general area that they all like the looks of, usually up a creek and always around plenty of rock, and will anchor the boat. Then they'll slip into their tubes and all go in different directions, working very close to specific areas along banks. They will fish with live crawfish, usually free lined or fished with only a split shot added to the line, and usually will catch a mess of catfish.

Hysmith emphasized that while seasonal migrations of larger cats lend themselves to fishing specific patterns and locations certain times of year, many small to medium-sized catfish of all three species pretty much stay put and can be caught virtually year 'round all along the edges of Lake Texoma.

"Throughout the lake, 12- to 20-inch catfish are not that big a deal to find and catch most of the time," he said.

Hysmith noted that Texoma's catfish populations appear quite stable. The population changes little from year to year, he said, and there are at least as many giant blues in the lake as there were 20 years ago.

The most recent creel survey, conducted in 1998, showed that the number of channel catfish released was roughly twice the number that had been harvested. Most catfish that get released are put back because they are under the legal harvest size (12 inches), Hysmith noted. A high release rate indicates an abundance of young fish, which suggests that the population is vibrant and healthy. By the same survey, harvested channel catfish ranged from 12 to 24 inches and averaged 14 inches.

Gillnet surveys were conducted in 2000. Of the catfish caught in those nets, 76 percent were at least 12 inches long. Channel catfish made up 69 percent of the same sample.

Hysmith admits that biologists still know only a little bit about Texoma's catfish. "Probably less than any other popular fish."

Gillnets, which are the main sampling tools, are 8 feet by 125 feet. Even with 30 of those spread out in different parts of the reservoir, that's not much net for 89,000 acres, Hysmith pointed out. "I also pay a lot of attention to what the fishermen are catching," he said.

While a lot remains to be learned, no one would question that Lake Texoma stands out as a premier catfishing destination.

Lake Texoma has a unique Lake Texoma Fishing License, which covers the entire lake for anyone, whether they are from Texas, Oklahoma, or neither. The license costs $7.50 in Texas or $7.75 in Oklahoma because of a difference in agent fee structures.

Catfishing regulations are consistent lakewide. The combined limit for blue and channel catfish is 25 fish, with a 12-inch minimum size. The limit for flatheads is five fish, with an 18-inch minimum size.

Mississippi River

When a rod surges down on James Patterson's boat, whoever dives for that rod had better be prepared to hold on tight. Big rivers yield big catfish, and James "Big Cat" Patterson does all of his catfishing on our nation's biggest river.

The world-record blue catfish, caught in 2001 by Charles Ashley Jr. of Marion, Arkansas, came from same section of the Mississippi River that Patterson plies. Ashley's incredible cat, which he caught on Spam, tipped the scales to 116 pounds, 12 ounces. He caught the giant cat within sight of the Interstate 55 bridge, which links Memphis, Tennessee, with West Memphis, Arkansas.

Farther down the mighty river, the Mississippi and Louisiana state-record blue catfish also came from the Mississippi River. The Mississippi state record, which was established in 1997 by Carroll Pearson, tipped the scales to 93 pounds. The Louisiana record, set the same year, was caught by Joseph Wiggins and weighed 105 pounds.

In addition to those fish that qualified for records, countless flatheads and blues of record proportions have been pulled from the Mississippi with trotlines and nets by commercial anglers. Veteran

Mississippi River anglers have little doubt that numerous world-record-size catfish remain in the river. The trick is getting the right fish to bite and then landing it.

Patterson, a Memphis fishing guide who targets catfish exclusively, has been fishing the mighty Mississippi for more than two decades. He has caught flatheads up to 60 pounds and blues up to 65. The day he caught his biggest blue, a second rod surged down just as he got the first fish into the boat. (Naturally, he was fishing alone that day.) After a second exhausting battle, he had a 62-pounder and a 65-pounder flopping around in the bottom of his boat.

The Mississippi River rises in northern Minnesota, not terribly far from the Canadian border. It begins as a stream that can be rock-hopped across but gains size and strength in a hurry. It borders on big-river proportions even by the time it exits Minnesota. Through the South, the Mississippi is a huge river by any measure. In many places, it is more than two miles wide.

At St. Louis, the Mississippi picks up the flow of the Missouri River, which heads up in western Montana. Downstream, the Ohio and the Arkansas Rivers add their enormous flows.

Patterson fishes approximately 50 miles of the Mississippi River, with Memphis setting close to the middle of that run. River conditions will cause him to run to spots at both ends of that range, but many of his biggest fish are caught within sight of downtown Memphis.

Because it drains nearly two-thirds of the nation, the lower Mississippi River can vary tremendously in character. A big snowstorm in the Rockies can affect Patterson's fishing in Memphis a couple of weeks later, and the river level commonly fluctuates 50 feet in a year. That means last week's hotspot might be high and dry—or completely washed out—this week. Like the water level, the river bottom changes continually, with sandbars, channels, oxbow openings, and deep holes constantly shifting.

Because of its size and its ever-changing character, the lower Mississippi doesn't get heavy fishing pressure in most places. Anglers are justifiably scared of a river that sometimes forms boat-sized whirlpools and carries floating forests as it churns toward the

Figure 25. James "Big Cat" Patterson, a full-time catfishing guide on the Mississippi River, has been fishing the Mississippi for more than 20 years.

Gulf of Mexico. They also know that the river's vastness can make
fish difficult to locate and catch.

Extensive shallow flats, which spread across much of the river
in many areas, don't hold many fish most of the time. To locate and
catch fish in the Mississippi, anglers have to learn how and when the
fish relate to specific types of features, like channel edges, riverbends,
sandbars, wing dikes, islands, and various kinds of shoreline cover.

Even within a specific river hole that catfish are holding in,
fishing conditions can change completely with only modest change
of the river level. A wing dike that has perfect current for a simple
setup one day may be unfishable the next day. Too much or too
little current can make it impractical or even impossible to anchor
the boat in a good position to lay out lines. Likewise, a current that
fish are relating to one day might be gone the next day because the
river has dropped even a few inches and is not spilling over the dike
the same way.

The Mississippi also connects with extensive backwaters, including dozens of oxbows. The backwater areas sometimes provide great fishing, especially when the river is raging, but they are as complex as the river itself. Some are connected at one or both ends, but only at certain water levels. They may or may not have current running through them, and they can range from drinking-water clear to flat-out muddy.

A lifelong catfishermen, Patterson learned to catch cats on the Tennessee River. When he moved to Memphis in the 1970s, he had to begin his education anew. It took several years before he began catching catfish consistently on the Mississippi.

Patterson fishes year-round on the Mississippi, adapting strategies as seasons and river conditions change. If pressed, he would probably admit that he likes late fall best, because that's when the river yields the most king-sized cats. Every season has its virtues on the Mississippi, however, and any time a rod goes down, the next world record could be at the other end of the line. Ashley's record catfish bit in heart of the dog days, on August 3.

The first few months of the year can be exceedingly tough or absolutely terrific. The tough part comes from often-high flows and quickly changing conditions. A fast rise in the river, brought about by a big winter storm, can shut down catfishing in a hurry. A hard front with harsh north winds blowing straight down the river can also become bitter enough to take the fun out of a day.

When the river is stable and the weather bearable, however, fishing is very predictable. Blues pile up in the deepest holes in the river, so Patterson can find huge concentrations of cats right where he expects them to be. Cats of all sizes move into refuge holes, so one fish may weigh 4 pounds and the next 40 pounds.

Large scour holes behind wing dams and along bluff banks offer the best winter prospects. Patterson spends a lot of time searching for concentrations of cats in big holes and then anchors upcurrent of the most fish. Because most holes have huge circling currents wrapping around them, upcurrent does not necessarily mean upstream. He rigs several lines with big chunks of cut skipjack, weighted heavily so they will stay on the bottom, and casts them downcurrent.

Some time around April, river temperatures moderate enough that the cats move out of their winter patterns. The river tends to run high through the spring, which pushes cats out of the channels and into shallow backwater areas along the river's edges. Patterson follows the fish shallow and fishes with small pieces of cut bait or shad guts, usually in less than 10 feet of water. He catches mostly channel catfish this way.

Flathead fishing can also be good during the spring. The flatheads will also move out of the main channel, especially if main-river currents get pushy. Flatheads will almost always be close to cover and generally will stay a bit deeper than channels. Patterson breaks out heavy gear and fishes big live gizzard shad around fallen trees or rockpiles for flatheads.

By July, the river usually runs down to a more manageable level, and the cats move back to the open water. Patterson fishes mostly for blues during the summer, often by drifting. The blues spread out over open-water areas that have uneven bottoms during the summer. Patterson drags three-way rigs and big chunks of skip-jack along the bottom.

Fall is big-fish time on the Mississippi River. Jumbo flatheads feed well until the water temperature dips below 50 degrees. Blues feed well right through the winter. During October and November, it's not uncommon for an angler to land a trophy flathead and a trophy blue in the same day. Fall also tends to bring the best water conditions of the year. The river typically is low, stable, and clearer than normal from September through some time in December.

Patterson generally will fish big live shad early and late in the day through the fall, with flatheads as his primary targets, and turn to cut skipjack through the middle of the day for big blues. Deep runs along riprap banks, edges of holes behind wing dams, and holes along riverbends are good areas for both species during the fall. Often, Patterson will fish live bait on a couple rods and cut bait on the rest at the same time.

About the time the flatheads stop hitting, late in the fall, the blues start moving deeper, sometimes within the same big holes, and becoming more concentrated. Soon they're back in the winter pattern and things have started over.

Patterson targets big cats most of the time, so he gears up accordingly. He matches Quantum Big Cat rods with Big Iron reels. The rods, which Patterson helped develop, have a lot of backbone. The reels are geared down for serious battles. He spools his reels with 50- to 75-pound Remington Power-Loct braided line. He does use lighter rods for drifting and lighter gear overall for shallow-water channel cats.

Patterson's bait of choice for blues is cut skipjack. For flatheads, he favors big live shad. Cut shad or skipjack do the job for channel catfish. He relies on frozen skipjack when fresh bait is not available and catches plenty of fish on them. Like most catfishermen, however, Patterson favors fresh skipjack. He catches his skipjack with small jigs on light spinning tackle and shad with a castnet.

Patterson cuts baitfish into big strips for blues and threads them on 7/O Eagle Claw Kahle hooks. For channels, he uses much smaller pieces of bait on 1/O or 2/O hooks. He uses three-way rigs, with 100-pound swivels and bank sinkers for most catfishing applications. Sinkers can range from a couple of ounces to 7 or 8 ounces, depending on the strength of the current and the depth of the water. He uses 40-pound-test Stren Catfish monofilament for leaders.

The Mississippi River runs through several states, even within the South, and licensing rules are sometimes complex, especially concerning backwaters. Therefore, it's essential that anglers take a good look at appropriate regulations booklets to make certain they are clear on where they can and cannot fish and on any other laws that would apply.

Also, it can't be stressed enough that the Mississippi River, even more so than most other waterways, demands caution at all times. Life jackets should be worn, not stowed. Powerful and unpredictable currents, large floating debris, hidden rockpiles, big waves and multi-ton barges are just a few of the hazards. Also, much of the Mississippi stays dangerously cold from mid-fall through mid-spring.

Missouri River

Rick Gebhardt used to fish for weeks without seeing another sport fisherman on the Missouri River. These days he expects to find the parking lot at his favorite ramp filled on any Saturday that brings decent weather, with many anglers targeting catfish. "There'll usually be 50 or 60 boats out there," he said.

Gebhardt, a catfish guide and highly successful catfish tournament angler, has fished for cats as long as he has been able to hold a fishing pole, and he has fished the Missouri River for more than 30 years. "When I first started fishing the Missouri, people said I was stupid to go out on that river. They thought it was too dangerous. Plus, no one knew just how many fish were in it," Gebhardt said.

Gebhardt noted that it was actually his mother who got him thinking about the Missouri River and the fish that certainly were in it. "Mother said, 'We need to fish that river,'" he recalled.

It didn't take Gebhardt long to figure out that the Missouri River was absolutely loaded with catfish. He caught almost nothing but channel cats for the first several years he fished the river, but over time he begin to unlock the secrets of the big blues, which he now targets almost exclusively.

The Missouri River rises high in the Rocky Mountains in western Montana and then cuts west-to-east across the state. Past Montana, the river either runs through or borders North Dakota, South Dakota, Nebraska, and Iowa before reaching its namesake state.

Big Muddy, as the lower Missouri River is commonly called, flows 553 miles through Missouri. By the time the river reaches Missouri, in the extreme northwestern corner of the state, it has gained big-river proportions by any standard, having picked up the flows of dozens of other rivers.

In Missouri, the river runs south to Kansas City, forming the border with Nebraska and then with Kansas. At Kansas City, the river's orientation turns east, and it cuts all the way across the state to St. Louis, where it joins forces with the Mississippi River.

The Missouri River offers good catfishing through most of its run; however, only the Missouri portion of the river could be considered part of the South. Of course, the best fishing for the biggest catfish is through the Missouri portion anyway, most anglers would agree.

The Missouri River reigns with little dispute as the premier big-cat destination in Missouri, with the Missouri portion of the Mississippi River being its only real rival. Supporting the Missouri River as the No. 1 pick, it produced the state's top flathead and blue catfish in the record books, both during the 1990s. The state-record

Figure 26. Catfish guide Rick Gebhardt (left) and Mark Davis of Shakespeare
Fishing are all smiles over a hefty Missouri River blue catfish. Photo
by J. T. Uptegrove.

blue, caught in 1991 by Clarence H. Kerr, weighed in at a hefty
103 pounds. The state-record flathead, caught in 1997 by Darrell
Hudspeth, weighed 77 pounds, 8 ounces.

Both fish are also listed as line-class world records in *Official
World and USA State Fresh Water Angling Records* (2002). Kerr's
record blue is the world record for 30-pound-test line. Hudspeth

easily established a line-class world record as he landed his giant flathead on 6-pound-test line!

Rounding out a "record book grand slam," the Missouri River also produced a line-class world-record channel catfish, albeit in Nebraska. The big channel, which was caught in 1983, weighed 35 pounds, 8 ounces, and set the world record for 8-pound-test line.

Beyond the big fish in the record books, the Missouri River has yielded dozens of triple-digit fish to commercial anglers and recreational trotliners. Just in the area around Glasgow, where Gebhardt lives and does most of his fishing, he could remember four 100-pound-plus fish having been caught in only a few years. The largest one bottomed out 100-pound scales, Gebhardt said, and he estimated it to weigh in the 130- to 140-pound range.

From a historical standpoint, no other American river—the Mississippi included—has more legends associated with it about catfish of absolutely enormous sizes. Captain Bill Heckman, a long-time riverboat pilot and steamboat historian, contended that cat-fish weighing between 125 and 200 pounds were common catches through the 1800s.

Telling of one legendary cat, Heckman said, "Of interest to fishermen is the fact that the largest known fish ever caught was taken just below Portland, Missouri. This fish, caught in 1866, was a blue channel cat and weighed 315 pounds. It provided the biggest sensation of those days all through Chamois and Morrison bottoms." (Heckman's accounts are reported in *Catfish 2000: Proceedings of the International Ictalurid Symposium*.)

Probably because of channelization projects, which forever changed the river's natural habitat, along with reduced water quality and extensive commercial fishing pressure, nothing even approach-ing those weights has been documented since the turn of the 20th century. The Missouri remains one of the nation's elite destinations for trophy catfish, however, and most anglers believe the fishing has been getting better in recent years.

In 1992, the state of Missouri banned all commercial harvest of catfish, as did several other states that the river cuts through. The fishing has improved dramatically since the change, almost all sport fishermen agree, and biologists' samples have shown larger average sizes. A survey conducted by the Missouri Conservation Department (MCD) revealed that the 79 percent of anglers who fished the river before and after the ban said fishing was better after 1993.

Gebhardt does the bulk of his fishing in the area around Glasgow, which is roughly halfway between Kansas City and St. Louis. Over the years, however, he has spent time fishing the entire Missouri portion. The overall character of the river is similar throughout Missouri, he said. It just gets bigger and bigger with each tributary picked up.

"The river is bigger, the wing dikes are longer, and the deep holes are deeper and larger," Gebhardt said of the lower river. He also noted that blue catfish become increasingly prevalent farther down the river. Downstream of Lexington, which is about 30 miles east of Kansas City, blues are the dominant cats, he said.

For several years after Gebhardt began fishing the Missouri River, he caught mostly channel catfish, with occasional small flatheads, fishing many of the same areas where he now loads up on jumbo blues. While Gebhardt has learned a lot of things about blue catfish behavior that help him target blues more effectively, the biggest difference that he can point to is the kind of bait he uses. Early on, he fished with dip baits, night crawlers, and strips of leopard frogs.

Somewhere along the way, Gebhardt began experimenting with cut bait, primarily cut gizzard shad, and when he did he began catching more blues. That led to using cut shad more often and baiting up with bigger pieces, which resulted in him catching more and larger blues. Eventually, he quit using anything other than big pieces of cut shad when blue catfish were his target species.

Gebhardt will occasionally fish with live shad, but usually only if the shad he catches are too small to cut into pieces or he is specifically targeting flatheads. He also uses Junnie's Cat Tracker dip bait when his clients want fast action from channel catfish. For big blues, though, he sticks with shad, which he usually cuts into three sections: head, body, and tail. He'll rig at least one rod with each type of cut and pay attention to which rods draw the hits.

"Invariably, one will be their preference any given day," Gebhardt said, "and you might as well bait 'em all that way for the rest of the day."

Gebhardt fishes the Missouri year 'round, unless the river freezes. In January, when the river is the coldest, he will fish primarily for channel catfish. By February, though, the big blues typically have begun feeding, and fishing action is sometimes fast. The big blues pile up in huge, deep holes and fairly calm water, which Gebhardt looks for behind wing dikes.

The deep holes, both around the dikes and on big outside bends, continue to play a big role in the fishing during March and April, but the fish begin moving out of the deepest parts of the holes, and rock banks also become important.

Early in May, the blues often get quite finicky for a week or two before they begin moving into their summer patterns. From late spring all the way through the summer, the best fishing is on flats, usually in 15 feet or less of water. As summer progresses, the fish move shallower. They also become much more nocturnal.

From the middle of May through October, Gebhardt does almost all his fishing under the stars. He will lay out several lines, with some in only a foot or two of water, set the clickers on the reels and lay down in the bottom of the boat.

Gebhardt said the first bite often won't occur for a couple of hours. He's not certain whether the fish get spooked when the boat moves over the shallow flat or whether it's just a matter of waiting for the right group of fish to come through.

"When they do hit, it can get wild," Gebhardt said. "Often we'll get three or four bites, one right after another. Those big blues are fun to hook in very shallow water."

Some time in October, the daytime fishing gets good again, and the fish start moving down the flats toward the edges of the deep holes. Through fall, the fish stay right along the edges of the holes. Once winter sets in, they drop down in the holes again. Gebhardt likes the cool—but not really cold—weather best. Throughout fall and in early spring, fishing for big blues can be outstanding in very predictable locations.

All along the Missouri River and throughout the seasons, wing dikes and hard bends in the river are the most important features because of the holes that form along them, according to Gebhardt. The fish relate to those features differently at different times of the year and under various conditions, but the waters around them always hold a lot of catfish.

Because of the size of the cats in the Missouri River and the strength of the river's currents, Gebhardt rigs up with heavy gear. He matches Shakespeare Ugly Stik Tiger Rods with Tidewater reels, spooled with 30-pound-test line. He uses basic Carolina rigs, typically weighted with 8-ounce egg weights and completed with 7/O Gamakatsu hooks.

Part of why there are so many enormous fish available to Gebhardt and other catfishermen on the Missouri is that the blues grow very quickly in the river. Gebhardt clips a certain spine from big cats that he catches and ships the spines to MCD biologists for aging.

144

A 75-pound blue catfish, which Gebhardt's brother caught while fishing with him, was only 14 years old, and several 40- to 50-pound fish Gebhardt has sent in spines from have been either 13 or 14 years old. "That's a lot of growing in that much time," he said.

Blue catfish often live more than 20 years, and they continue to grow all their lives, so it's easy to see the potential that still exists. Missouri River catfish may never again reach the sizes they are said to have grown to in the 1800s and before, but the Missouri undoubtedly possesses the potential to rewrite the record books.

Gebhardt noted that while the Missouri River is not as daunting as he was once warned, its strong currents and hidden obstructions do present hazards that anglers must be aware of. If anglers understand buoy makers and boating rules, know how to read the water's surface and remain aware of wing dikes, they are unlikely to encounter problems, he said.

Ohio River

If anyone ever doubted the Ohio River's position among the South's premier catfisheries, Bruce Midkiff of Owensboro, Kentucky, answered all questions in 1999 when he wrestled a new Kentucky/ Indiana state-record blue from the river.

It wasn't enough for Midkiff to land a 104-pound catfish. When he finally got giant fish into his boat, he had to pry another deeply bent and throbbing rod from its holder and fight a second fish. When all was said and done, Midkiff had a 50-pound blue catfish flopping beside a 104-pound blue catfish in the bottom of his boat.

The Ohio River, which officially begins in Pittsburgh, Pennsylvania, at the confluence of the Allegheny and Monongahela Rivers, flows roughly 1,000 miles before emptying into the Mississippi River. The Ohio gathers waters from 11 different states and makes up 20 percent of the Mississippi River's watershed. Through the lower end of the Ohio River's run, portions spread more than a mile across.

The Ohio River also supports a tremendous amount of catfish food, with gizzard shad and skipjack herring being found in big numbers throughout the river, along with threadfin shad through the lower reaches. In addition, crawfish and various mollusk provide forage for some cats, while nearly every kind of fish that swims in the river sometimes shows up on the flathead menu.

The Ohio River produces channel, flathead, and blue catfish, all in good numbers and all reaching large sizes. Flatheads and channels can be found anywhere along the river's course. Blues are only found through the lower half of the big river.

Blue catfish show up on occasion in samples and on the ends of fishermen's lines beginning around Capt. Anthony Meldahl Lock and Dam, which is just upstream of Cincinnati, according to Doug Hendley, the fisheries biologist over the Ohio River for the Kentucky Department of Fish and Wildlife Resources. Blues become a significant part of the fishing picture somewhere around Louisville. Continuing down the river, they become increasingly abundant.

Interestingly, blue catfish appear to be expanding their range up the Ohio River system, according to Hendley, which he believes may be attributable to a couple of main factors. First, the Ohio River has been cleaned up significantly over the past several years. In addition, zebra mussels are now established through much of the river, and blues seem able to make good use of zebra mussels as forage.

The Ohio River that anglers see today differs significantly in character from what once existed. In its natural state, the river alternated between shoals and pools, with shoaled sections being shallow, swift, and in many cases unnavigable. In 1820, a commission of

Figure 27. Bruce Midkiff used a special livewell constructed from a horse-feeding trough to keep the Kentucky/Indiana state-record blue catfish in good condition and was able to release it back into the Ohio River after having it properly weighed and identified. Photo courtesy of Bruce Midkiff.

Ohio River Valley state representatives identified 102 navigational obstructions along the river's route and attained federal funding to begin remedying the problem.

Early efforts included dredging sandbars, removing snags, cutting a channel and building numerous low lock-and-dam structures. Those dams were eventually replaced by 20 high-rise lock-and-dam structures, which remain in place today.

The locks and dams divide the river into pools, with short tailwater sections below each dam. They create a river that is generally lazy and deep, especially through the lower reaches of each pool. Some current pushes all the way through each pool, however.

Catfishing is very popular on the Ohio River. Creel surveys conducted at the Newburgh and Cannelton locks and dams showed catfish making up 20 and 21 percent of the harvested catch from the respective tailwaters.

Pools make up 99 percent of the Ohio River, but most catfish anglers devote the bulk of their time to fishing tailwater sections. There is good reason for that. "Tailwaters are fish concentrators," Hendley said. "Especially during and after the spawn, from late spring all the way through the summer, the catfish really get concentrated in the tailwaters."

Most locks and dams also offer at least some measure of shoreline access, according to Hendley. However, he noted that some require more initiative than others to access, and fishermen are not always within casting range of the best waters for big cats. "Each one is a little bit different," he noted.

Hendley said that boating provides anglers the best opportunity to hook into big catfish. Anglers who fish tailwaters by boat are able to fish right over the best-looking spots, which makes it much easier to present baits in sometimes-strong currents without repeatedly getting snagged.

All of the locks and dams have similar fish-holding appeal, according to Hendley. He pointed toward the Markland and Cannelton tailwaters as traditionally popular catfishing destinations.

Markland Lock and Dam, locate between Louisville and Cincinnati, attracts anglers who seek jumbo-sized flatheads. However, channel cats, which abound in this tailwater, should not be overlooked.

Part of what makes Markland extra productive is that it was built immediately upstream of one of the river's original lock-and-dam structures. The old blown-out structure lies right in the tailwater, providing fabulous holding areas for catfish, according to Hendley. Flatheads, which like a break in the current and specific structural features to relate to, will hold in the debris from the old structure.

Cannelton Lock and Dam, located upstream of Owensboro, produces all three species in big numbers and big sizes. Jumbo blues are its trademark, however. Bruce Midkiff was fishing an 80-foot deep hole in the Cannelton tailwater when he hooked into his record-breaking blue catfish.

During the summer, blue and flathead catfish move right up into the boils below the dam and feed heavily on shad and herring, according to Hendley. Fishermen catch a lot of giant cats each summer while fishing live bait near the dam for stripers. Anglers who target jumbo cats use both live and dead shad and herring and often fish quite close to the dam. The Smithland Lock and Dam and Lock and Dam 52, next in the system, are hotspots for trophy-sized blues.

While tailwaters concentrate cats and make prime locations very easy to recognize, many other areas in the pools and in embayments off the main river hold catfish. The best spots outside the tailwaters depend largely on the season and on what kind of cat an angler wants to target.

Because blues like current and room to roam, they are apt to be found in any big, deep hole that has current pushing through it. Prime spots are on deep outside bends, where the river pushes into mountainsides and creates big bluff holes.

River and creek mouths and channel edges inside of embayments often hold big concentrations of channel catfish during the summer. Channels will hold on good structure throughout a pool, in fact, based on Hendley's observations. As summer melds to fall, channel catfish will often move quite close to the banks and hold in very shallow water, he said.

Flathead catfish use some of the same bluff holes as blues do during the summer. However, they are more apt to be right against the bank, instead of out in the hole, especially if eroding banks have caused trees to fall into the water along the edges. Historic lock-and-dam structures all along the river also provide good holding areas for flatheads, as do the confluences of tributaries with the main river. Like channels, flathead generally move quite a bit shallower during the fall.

Hendley offered one final tip regarding where the most cats are apt to be found. He suggested that anglers probe waters around any grain-loading facility along the river. "Sometimes they get a little sloppy loading the grain, and the catfish can really get concentrated," he said.

Bruce Midkiff, who passed away in late 2001, targeted trophy-caliber flatheads and blues whenever he fished for catfish. His biggest cat, prior to landing the 104-pounder, was a 59-pound blue, and he caught dozens of 40-pound-plus flathead and blue catfish from the river.

Midkiff fished in the tailwaters and in deep river holes—the deepest he could find—throughout the pools. He fished mostly in the Cannelton and Newburgh tailwaters and the Newburgh pool, largely because that section is closest to where he lived. Some of the holes he liked best are quite close to Owensboro.

Midkiff believed in the big-bait/big-fish philosophy. He fished with cut and live gizzard shad and skipjack, and he thought nothing of putting down a bait that was more than a foot long and weighed as much as a pound. Because of the river's often-strong currents, the depths Midkiff often fished, and the size of the fish the Ohio River produces, he used a lot of weight, 50-pound-test line, and stout gear.

Arguably, the most intriguing piece of equipment that Midkiff carried was his livewell, which, like his other gear, was designed for big fish. Midkiff's livewell, which was constructed from a horse-watering trough, allowed him to release his state-record fish six hours after he caught it, after it had been properly weighed and identified.

Anglers who fish quite close to lock-and-dam structures typically look for seams between strong current lines and eddies and put baits down with heavily weighted three-way rigs. Big live gizzard shad are the bait of choice for flatheads, most tailwater fishermen agree. Two- or 3-inch-wide strips of cut skipjack offer better bets for blue catfish. Smaller skipjack strips or threadfin shad, cut in half, do the job nicely for smaller blues or channel catfish.

Downstream of tailwaters, where rock jumbles become less abundant and currents are not quite as strong, anglers can get by with simpler rigs. Anglers targeting blues or channels typically anchor upstream of the waters they want to fish, cast their lines down into the hole, allow them to settle on the bottom and set the rods in holders. They use simple Carolina rigs with whatever amount of weight it takes to hold their offerings in place.

Cut skipjack remains the bait of choice for blue catfish. A variety of baits, including commercial stink baits, shrimp, and chicken livers, will work well for channel catfish.

Whether they fish in tailwaters or in pools and whether they target blues, channels, or flatheads, many serious Ohio River catfishermen turn mostly to nighttime fishing through the heart of the summer.

Like all large rivers, the Ohio River presents major hazards, and caution is essential. Deceptively powerful currents, extremely shallow water outside of channels, rough water on windy days, large floating debris, and turbulent water below dams are just some of the hazards. Boaters should be familiar with safe boating practices, and life jackets should be worn any time a boat is moving and at all times below lock-and-dam structures.

Santee Cooper

Any time a rod goes down at Santee Cooper, the fish at the other end may weigh 6 pounds or 60 pounds, according to Joe Drose, a lifelong fisherman on South Carolina's most famous fishing hole and legendary guide who targets catfish almost exclusively.

The catfishery that some anglers consider the world's finest produces big blues, flatheads, and channels throughout the year, according to Joe's brother, Don Drose, who likewise has been fishing the Santee Cooper Lakes all his life and has been guiding full-time for more than 35 years.

Flatheads must pull the scales to at least 40 pounds to earn trophy recognition in Santee Cooper country, and even 50-pound catfish don't garner much special attention. Dozens of full-time guides earn a large part of their living guiding anglers to Santee Cooper's trophy-caliber flatheads and blues. Santee Cooper stands out in the record books for having produced the all-tackle world-record channel catfish, a 58-pound giant caught in 1964 by W. B. Whaley.

The Cooper River, in its tailwater portion below the Santee Cooper Lakes, yielded a 109-pound, 5-ounce blue catfish in 1991 that established the all-tackle world record at the time. The record fell a few years later, but the fish remains in the books as the line-class world record for 16-pound-test and as South Carolina's state record.

The Diversion Canal, which links the two lakes, produced South Carolina's state-record flathead, completing Santee Cooper's record-book slam. Caught in 2001 by Jessica Preston of Gilbert, South Carolina, the fish weighed in at 79 pounds, 4 ounces. The previous state-record flathead had also come from the Division Canal—only a month earlier.

Of the three major catfish species, only channels are native to South Carolina waters. Flatheads and blues were stocked only once, with a modest number of each having been put in the lakes in the mid-1960s. While the two exotic species now dominate the lake and have displaced a lot of channel catfish mass, some really big channels still come from the same waters that produced the largest one ever.

The Santee Cooper system is commonly referred to as Santee Cooper Lake or Santee Cooper Reservoir, but either is a misnomer. The system, which includes more than 170,000 acres, consists of two lakes—Lake Marion and Lake Moultrie—and the system of rivers and canals that feed, connect and drain the lakes. The lakes were built on the Santee and Cooper Rivers in the 1940s and are operated for power generation by the Santee Cooper Corporation.

Lake Marion is long, fairly narrow, and quite shallow through its upper end. The entire lake is loaded with cypress and tupelo trees, but through the lower half of the lake, the trees are permanently flooded and dead, and far more timber lies hidden 20 feet beneath the surface than what is visible from above water.

Lake Moultrie is open and bowl shaped, with all of its swampy areas along the edges. It covers cleared forests, farmland, and swamps, and has networks of ditches and roadbeds underneath it. Navigation is far easier on Moultrie than Marion, but finding fish can be difficult because most of the structure lies well beneath the surface and far from any landmarks.

No single, simple answer explains why Santee Cooper has remained so productive through the years despite extensive pressure from recreational and especially commercial fishermen. It is extraordinarily fertile, and its forage base is very diverse. Abundant freshwater mussels provide important food for channel and blue catfish, as do threadfin and gizzard shad, blueback herring, and menhaden. Flatheads eat everything that swims, including good populations of white perch, various sunfish species, and young catfish.

One of the real appeals of fishing for Santee Cooper cats is that the action remains interesting throughout the year. Because the system is diverse and all three major species are well represented, veteran anglers learn to alter their approaches through the seasons and take advantage of the best fishing available.

Through late winter and early spring, blue catfish tend to move shallow, and Don Drose can often be found anchored within

152

Figure 28. Joe Drose, left, has lived beside the Santee Cooper lakes all his life and has never done any work other than guiding on the two big lakes. Drose has guided almost exclusively for catfish for the past several years.

casting range of Lake Marion's banks. Most of his lines will be stretched out toward the shore, usually fanned across a clay point.

"People don't think of catfish in shallow water, especially during winter," Don said, "but these fish do move shallow every year, and it's a lot of fun when they do."

The cats stack up in the shallow water as strong winds from cold fronts beat the banks, which causes them to muddy up and therefore to warm faster than surrounding waters anytime the sun beats down. The wind also breaks off mussels and washes plankton into the shallow water, which schools of baitfish follow.

Wind direction, water color, bank makeup, and the presence of mussels and baitfish, therefore, are all key factors for identifying shorelines to set up near. Don does most of his looking along the edge of the main lake and at the mouths of major creeks.

Don uses a simple rig, with a 1-ounce, elongated weight, an 18-inch leader, and a 5/0 Eagle Claw hook to lay out flatlines in the shallow water. Usually setting up close to a point so he can cover a range of conditions, he will spread pieces of shad and herring from right against the bank down through depths of about 10 feet.

Many veteran Santee Cooper anglers consider March 1 the unofficial beginning of the trophy catfish season, simply because that is when the season opens for commercial harvest of big, ocean-run blueback herring, the classic bait for giant blue catfish. How-ever, Don likes to get a head start on the action by going out at night and netting foot-long gizzard shad, which are big and oily, just like the big bluebacks.

The two biggest catfish Don has brought into his boat, each stretching the scales to 81 pounds, were caught during February. Interestingly, the two giant fish were caught almost exactly one year apart, and from the same GPS coordinates. (Sorry, that's as specific as Don will get!) Joe's biggest blue, a 75-pounder, also hit during February.

Big bluebacks or gizzards are cut into thick strips early in the spring, and Don and Joe will lay them out on flatlines in areas that have produced king-sized blues in recent days or past years.

Finding the big blues begins with finding bait over humps or other good structure. Areas around the main Santee River channel in lower Lake Marion, near the spillways at Santee Dam and through the Diversion Canal, are all worth searching.

As spring sets in, the flatheads also become active, so Don will often set out a few lines for them. The latter part of March through the first couple of weeks of April is the most likely time of the year to catch trophy-sized flatheads and blues in the same trip, Don noted.

Early in the year, white perch work well for flatheads. Don typically finds flatheads in the river channel, but the blues are more apt to hold on top of the ledge. To target both species, he will often anchor over the river channel, dropping lines rigged with live bait straight down and fishing them just off the bottom. He will then cast flatlines rigged with big pieces of cut bait onto the ledge.

Because of the size of Santee Cooper's biggest flatheads and blues, and because of the thousands of fallen trees that litter Lake Marion's bottom, Don does all his catfishing with 130-pound Spiderwire braided line. He uses fairly large conventional reels on Shakespeare Wonder Rods, which he contends a fish simply cannot break.

Joe does a lot of his late-spring catfishing with Junnie's Cat Tracker dip baits. His spring patterns were revolutionized several years ago by 40 catfish in three hours, all caught on the dip bait during the filming of a TV show. "There were five other guide boats around us," Joe said, "and they weren't catching a thing using small blueback herring, which is the same bait I normally would have been using that time of year."

Joe turns to the Cat Tracker baits from late April through the end of June because that is when a lot of water is flowing through the Santee Cooper Lakes and particularly through the canals that link and drain the lakes. Current, he explained, is essential to the effectiveness of the dip bait.

Through much of the year, Joe spends a lot of days drifting on Lake Moultrie. He begins by searching with his electronics, a Humminbird graph, and GPS unit. "Prior to Hurricane Hugo, there were plenty of trees along the shores to line up with and find spots in the middle of the lake, but now you almost need GPS," Joe said. "You can be 20 feet in front of a ditch that cats are holding in, and you could just as well be across the lake from it."

Joe knows the bottom of Lake Moultrie better than most folks know their own backyards, so he uses the GPS to lead him quickly to inundated ditches, hills, swamps, and so on, that he expects to hold fish. Then, he turns to the graph to look for baitfish and catfish before beginning a drift.

Joe uses bottom-bumping rigs that consist of a pencil weight, leader and hook, and a cork pegged halfway down the leader. Threading blueback herring, threadfin shad, or menhaden on to 5/O hooks, Joe runs his baits a long way back before engaging his Shakespeare Tidewater Reels, which are matched with Ugly Stik Tiger Rods.

Joe mostly drifts through the summer while Don continues targeting flatheads. The flatheads bite well through the summer, especially early and late in the day, but finding them becomes a greater challenge because many of the best deep-water areas don't maintain high enough dissolved oxygen levels for the cats. Bluegills become the most productive bait for flatheads through the dog days.

Fall is prime time for big flatheads on the Santee Cooper Lakes. Fishermen may still lay out a flatline or two rigged with cut bait for blue catfish, but trophy flatheads become the primary targets. Big fish will pile up on good structure along inundated river channels, and fishermen who are set up over good holes when the big flatheads decide to feed may be in for a treat.

Don had a regular client aboard one day, and they had been setting up over decent fish for roughly 45 minutes at a time. They were locating catfish, but no good concentrations, until they pulled over a hole and marked a dozen big fish, all very close together. They set up on that spot for 2½ hours before the first fish hit. Once the action began, however, it didn't stop until they had boated 16 flatheads, 11 of which weighed more than 40 pounds.

Winter yields fast action from blue cats. The cats stack up, usually in December, and when they do, it becomes almost impossible to keep more than one line per angler baited at any given time.

Cold weather narrows the comfort zone of blueback herring and threadfin shad, which forces virtually all the baitfish to pile up in the deepest water around the dams of the two lakes. "The baitfish get so thick that they blacken the screen, and you can't see beneath them," Joe said. "But when there is that much bait, you don't need to see anything else. The catfish are down there."

Joe and Don will catch their bait from the same place they plan to fish, usually with cast nets. Often stringing two or three baits on each hook, they will drop lines to just below the schools of baitfish and engage the reels. Those baits don't tend to stay there long.

Don catches most of his concentrated cats from Lake Marion, either anchoring or using his trolling motor to work slowly along the dam. Joe typically sticks with Lake Moultrie, working the deep water around the powerhouse. Fishing Moultrie, Joe finds a fair number of channels mixed in with the blues, and they are almost always big, by channel catfish standards.

Extreme cold can cause a winter kill of baitfish, and the catfish will go into a frenzy as the dying baitfish practically fall into their open mouths. After any such winter kill, however, the cats will be "fat and happy" and mighty tough to catch for a few weeks.

With or without a winter kill, fast action around the dam fades as waters begin to warm in different parts of the lake and the big concentrations of baitfish disperse. Of course, that brings us back to where we started, to the point where the blue catfish are about to move shallow.

Tennessee River

Tom Evans and Gary Garth were only trying to get their lines in at the end of the day. They had hauled in more than 200 pounds of catfish in only a few hours and were ready to call it a day. The cats weren't ready to quit, however. They were grabbing baits and running off with them faster than the two anglers could get their lines out of the water. A half an hour and close to 100 extra pounds later, the tired fishermen were finally were able to rest.

The day before, I had been in the boat with Evans, along with Mark Wiese of Toccoa, Georgia. We had caught and released a couple hundred pounds of blue catfish ourselves, including numerous 20-pound-plus fish and a couple that broke the 40-pound mark. A few weeks prior, I had spent another day in the boat with Evans, and we had caught more than a dozen cats, five of which weighed more than 30 pounds.

Evans, a fishing guide and photographer, lives in Loudoun, just a mile or so from the Tennessee River. He had been telling me for several weeks about all the catfish he had been catching. When I finally got to the river to fish with him, I found that it was every bit as good as he assured me it would be—if not better. At one point on each day I was in the boat with Evans, we had two 30-pound-plus fish bouncing around in the boat at the same time, simply because there was no time to unhook one before we both got busy tying to land another.

From late spring well into the fall, Evans catches catfish practically every time he goes out. He and his clients have caught dozens of catfish over 30 pounds, plenty over 40, and more than a handful that have topped the 50-pound mark.

And then there were those fish that they could never turn!

"I just can't get a grasp on how many huge fish there must be in this river," Evans said. "Any time a fish hits, that fish could be the next world record."

Waters that collect to head up the Tennessee River rise in the mountains of southwestern Virginia, East Tennessee, western North Carolina, and North Georgia. The river officially begins just east of Knoxville, where the Holston and French Broad Rivers join forces at the head of Fort Loudoun Lake. Both tributaries are large flows, so the Tennessee River is a major river from its beginning point.

Beginning at Fort Loudoun, the Tennessee River runs its course through a series of nine major impoundments, built both for flood control and for hydroelectric power generation. West of Knoxville it enters Watts Bar Lake and turns southwesterly, toward Chattanooga, and goes through Chickamauga and Nickajack Lakes.

Just downstream of Nickajack Dam, the river dips into Alabama, where it goes through Guntersville, Wheeler, and Wilson Lakes and enters Pickwick Lake. At the lower end of Pickwick, the river, now flowing south to north, re-enters Tennessee. Finally, it backs into Kentucky Lake, a massive impoundment that is divided between Tennessee and Kentucky. Downstream of Kentucky Lake, the Tennessee River completes its run as it pours into the Ohio River not far from where the Ohio feeds the mighty Mississippi.

The entire length of the Tennessee River is a world-class catfish fishery. A recent former state-record blue catfish came from Fort

Figure 29. Tom Evans, a Tennessee River guide who lives just outside Knoxville, catches tremendous numbers of heavyweight cats from the big
river during the summer.

Loudoun, and a previous all-tackle world record blue came from the
Alabama portion of the Tennessee River. Line-class world records
for blue catfish include five fish from the Tennessee River.

Additionally, countless triple-digit-weight cats have been pulled
from the river by commercial anglers over the years. Commercial
fishing is no longer permitted in the upper part of the river, which
closely relates to one reason that the catfishing is so good.

Severe fish-consumption restrictions, including a recommendation to avoid all catfish consumption in some waters, keeps catfishing pressure very light in the Knoxville area. Of the few anglers who do specifically target catfish in this area, most heed the warning and put all cats back in the river.

It is unfortunate that anglers who want to take home a few catfish don't have that opportunity on parts of the Tennessee River, and the fact that those warnings exist does not speak well for how the river has been cared for. Those things acknowledged, increasing numbers of anglers value catfish even more for the sport they offer than for their eating qualities and put most cats back, whether they can eat the fish or not. For anyone who doesn't care about keeping cats, the trophy fishery on the Tennessee River is truly outstanding.

Far beyond any benefits derived from a forced catch-and-release situation, the Tennessee River produces big cats because it offers first-rate big-cat habitat. Big catfish like big rivers, with plenty of room to spread out, vast shallow flats, and deep holes and current they can relate to.

They also require lots and lots of food. The Tennessee River is extremely fertile and supports a tremendous forage base. Gizzard shad, threadfin shad, and skipjack herring provide abundant forage for blues. In addition there are crawfish, various mollusks, and numerous other kinds of fish that cats feed on.

The Tennessee River produces big cats of all three popular species. Blues, however, dominate the big-cat scene. Evans, like most anglers who specifically target trophy catfish in the river, catches far more blues than channels or flatheads. The river does support an excellent population of flatheads, with some absolute giants in the mix. However, fishing for them calls for different strategies.

Evans does most of his catfishing in the upper end of Watts Bar Lake, along the main Tennessee River channel. However, having experimented a bit with the fertile waters of Fort Loudoun, the Clinch River arm of Watts Bar, and various other points along the Tennessee River, he is convinced he would find similar success in other parts of the river. Those beliefs are well backed by the consistent big-cat success enjoyed by other serious catfishermen on other parts of the Tennessee River. Evans fishes the stretch that he does most of the time primarily because of convenience.

Upstream of where Evans fishes, Fort Loudoun Lake is known to produce gigantic catfish, and it may get less catfishing pressure than any other stretch of Tennessee River. Beyond creek mouths and big bends in the Tennessee River, deep holes up the Holston River and French Broad River arms yield massive catfish.

Farther down the river, in Chickamauga Lake, the area around the confluence of the Hiwassee River with the Tennessee River is known to produce a lot of big catfish. Local anglers like to drift across flats, especially those that are adjacent to the old river channel, with cut bait bounced along the bottom.

Farther down, the Chickamauga and Nickajack tailwaters both offer very good prospects. One of the best things about the tail-waters is that bank-fishermen enjoy a good opportunity to hook into a big catfish. Tennessee Valley Authority maintains good bank-access areas around the tailwaters of all the Tennessee River impound-ments. Boating anglers do best with cut bait and three-way rigs fished fairly near the dam.

Wheeler Lake, in the Alabama portion, yielded the former all-tackle world record and has produced numerous triple-digit fish to commercial fishermen. The tailwaters of Wheeler and Wilson dams, meanwhile, yield outstanding catfishing for channels, blues and flatheads.

Turning back into Tennessee, the Pickwick tailwater is some-times called the Catfishing Capital of the World, and a big catfishing festival and tournament are held here every year. Cats of all sizes abound in this tailwater, and catfishing is very popular. In the river-ine portion between Pickwick Dam and the more open waters of the Kentucky Lake, there are long stretches of river that get very little pressure because they are not convenient to very many anglers. Deep holes through these areas produce some huge catfish every year.

Evans does most of his catfishing in a section of river that begins approximately 5 miles downstream of Fort Loudoun Dam and extends to the mouth of the Clinch River. He fishes dozens of holes, all of which have the common denominator of deep water that is close to relatively shallow water. Most are along outside bends in the river, where bluff banks continue well below the surface and drop into deep water. A few are open-water ledges.

Current is a major factor that helps Evans determine which hole to start on and where to set up along it. He has found a good flow and active cats go hand-in-hand, and different holes have good current running across them at different water levels. Because the river can run at such a broad range of levels, Evans often has to go look at several holes in order to find one that has suitable current pushing across it.

Sometimes the water is simply is not flowing well when Evans gets to the river. He will still fish, but he doesn't expect the action to get good until some current starts flowing. "The more current, the better the fishing," Evans said.

Evans fishes exclusively with fresh, cut skipjack. He has experimented with shad and a couple of other kinds of bait. However, nothing has come close to rivaling the effectiveness of skipjack. He discards the head and tail sections of his baitfish, having had minimal success with either, and cuts the remaining part into 1- to 2-inch strips. He will also use the skipjack's "guts" as a separate bait.

"The line with the guts on it almost always gets hit first," Evans said, "but it is usually a channel catfish or a small blue."

Evans uses basic Carolina rigs on all his lines, usually with 2 ounces of weight. For hooks, he uses either heavy-grade 6/O or 7/O bait hooks or 10/O to 12/O circle hooks. He uses heavy-action fiberglass rods and clicker-type baitcasting reels, which he spools with 40-pound-test Silver Thread line. He uses 100-pound-test leader between his swivel and his hook because of abrasion from the catfish's teeth.

He casts each bait downstream, lets it settle on the bottom, and then puts the rod in a holder with the spool open but the reel's clicker on. He doesn't pay attention to nibbles that wiggle rod tips or cause the clickers to make staccato yelps. He waits for the screaming runs, which inevitably come. When a reel starts yelling for help, he lifts the rod from the holder, throws the reel into gear as he lunges back against the fish, and holds on tight.

Fresh bait is essential to good catfishing, Evans has found, and sometimes catching skipjack presents a bigger challenge than catching catfish. Evans always persists, though, and doesn't stop collecting bait until he has at least a half-dozen big skipjack in his cooler.

Once he gets set up on a good catfishing hole and reel click-ers start screaming, the last thing an avid catfisherman like Tom Evans wants is to have to pull anchor, leave that spot, and go out searching for more bait.

Because fish-consumption advisories vary immensely from lake to lake along the Tennessee River, anglers should be certain to look at specific listings before keeping any fish to take home.

Catfish Guides Referenced

Jerry Crook, Tennessee River, (205) 608-0933,
www.alabamaoutdoors.net/tailrace.html

Don Drose, Santee Cooper, (888) 478-2536

Joe Drose, Santee Cooper, (800) 858-7018,
www.santeecoopercats.com

Tom Evans, Tennessee River, (865) 604-9233,
www.tomevansoutdoors.com

Rick Gebhardt, (660) 338-2340, www.rickgebhardt.com

Donny Hall, Cumberland/Tennessee rivers, (615) 383-4464

James Patterson, Mississippi River, (901) 383-8674,
www.bigcatfishing.com

Randolph's Landing, Santee Cooper, (800) BIG CATS,
www.randolphs-landing.com

Glenn Stubblefield, Kentucky Lake, (270) 436-5584,
(731) 642-2828

Keith Sutton, Amazon River Basin, (501) 847-9643,
www.ccoutdoors.com

Jackie Vancleave, Reelfoot Lake, (877) BLUE BANK,
www.bluebankresort.com

State Record Catfish

Alabama

Blue	111.0	William McKinley	Lake Wheeler
Channel	40.0	Donald R. Cox	Inland Lake
Flathead	80.0	Rick Conner	Alabama River
White	10.5	Roy T. Britton	Chambers County Public Lake
Bullhead	3.13	Charles A. Lane	Private Pond

Arkansas

Blue*	116.12	Charles Ashley Jr.	Mississippi River
Channel	38.0	Joe Holleman	Lake Ouachita
Flathead	80.0	Wesley White	Arkansas River
Black Bullhead	4.12	Janet Story	Point Remove Creek

Florida

Blue	61.5	Vincent R. Walston	Little Escambia Creek
Channel	44.5	Joe Purvis	Lake Bluff
Uncertified Flathead	48.4	Bobby Simmons	Escambia River
Flathead	57.5	Tom Norman	Hillsboro River
White	18.88	Jim Miller	Withlacoochee River
Brown Bullhead	5.72	Robert Bengis	Cedar Creek

Georgia

Blue	62.0	Ralph H. Barbee Jr.	Clarks Hill Lake
Channel	44.12	Bobby Smithwick	Altamaha River
Flathead	67.8	Gene Middleton	Altamaha River
White	8.10	James Sanders	Savannah River
Brown Bullhead	5.8	James Andrews	O. F. Veal Pond

Kentucky

Blue	104.0	Bruce Midkiff	Ohio River
Channel	28.3	Hope Tinsley	Farm Pond
Flathead	97.0	Esker Carroll	Green River
Bullhead	5.3	Harry Case	Guist Creek Lake

Louisiana

Blue	105.0	Joseph Wiggins	Mississippi River
Channel	30.31	Harold W. Clubb	Canal
Flathead	66.0	Harley Rakes	Red River

Mississippi

Blue	93.0	Carrol Pearson	Mississippi River
Channel	51.12	Tom Edwards	Lake Tom Bailey
Flathead	65.8	Wade Arnold	Pickwick Lake
Black Bullhead	5.56	Harold B. Alexander	Sunrise Lake
Brown Bullhead*	6.13	Bobby L. Gibson	Farm Pond
Yellow Bullhead	2.13	Robert Cason	Mossy Lake

Missouri

Blue	103.0	Clarence H. Kerr	Missouri River
Channel	34.10	Gerald Siebenmorgen	Lake Jacomo
Flathead	77.8	Darrell Hudspeth	Missouri River
Black Bullhead	4.11	Ron Miller	Binder Lake
Brown Bullhead	3.3	Greg Clanahan	Loch Loma Lake
Yellow Bullhead	5.13	J. D. Hall	Farm Pond

North Carolina

Blue	80.0	Keith Davis	Cape Fear River
Channel	40.8	P. P. Paine	Fontana Lake
Flathead	69.0	Edward C. Davis	Cape Fear River
White	13.0	Jerry Wayne Bentley	Lake James
Brown Bullhead	3.12	Gregory Dale Hughes	Buck Hall Creek

South Carolina

Blue	109.4	George A. Lijewski	Tailrace Canal
Channel *	58.0	W. H. Whaley	Lake Moultrie
Flathead	79.4	Jessica Preston	Diversion Canal
White	9.15	Jim Schwietert	Lake Murray
Bullhead	6.3	Dorothy Dewitt	Edisto River

Tennessee

Blue	112.0	Robert E. Lewis	Cumberland River
Channel	41.0	Clint Walters Jr.	Fall Creek Falls Lake
Flathead	85.15	Larry Kaylor	Hiwassee River
Black Bullhead	3.5.5	Hunter Chance Gaither	Embertons Pond
Brown Bullhead	2.14	John T. Hammond	Lake Chickamauga
Yellow Bullhead	4.8	Jessie R. Johnson	Lake Chickamauga

Texas

Blue	100.0	Reyes Martinez	Lake Texoma
Channel	36.5	Mrs. Joe L. Cockrell	Pedernales River
Flathead	98.5	James Laster	Lake Palestine
Black Bullhead	4.02	Roy Calame	Navarro Mills Lake
Yellow Bullhead	3.2	Herschell Spears	Lake Fork

Virginia

Blue	71.12	Hugh L. Self Jr.	James River
Channel	31.8	Sue Stanley	Rappahannock River
Flathead	66.4	Mike Willems	Occoquan Reservoir
White	7.6	Thomas F. Elkins	Western Branch Reservoir

West Virginia

Channel	21.25	Mike C. Mace	Lee Creek
Flathead	70.0	L. L. McClung	Little Kanawha River
Bullhead	6.1	Gary R. Freeman	Tygart Lake

*World Record

Catfish Recipes

Baked Catfish Fillets
(for the health-conscious)

Mike & Carol Marsh

Olive oil
1 mild white onion
2 mild green banana peppers or 1 bell pepper
½ teaspoon salt
¼ teaspoon pepper
¼ teaspoon turmeric
½ teaspoon parsley flakes
2 pounds of catfish fillets

Heat oven to 350 degrees. Coat 11 x 7 baking dish with just enough oil to cover bottom of dish. Brush fillets lightly with oil. Dust fillets with salt, pepper, turmeric, and parsley, and then arrange in dish so none are touching. Slice peppers and onions into thin rings and place over fillets. Thin slicing allows the rings to wilt when baked, making contact with the fish. For bell peppers cut rings in half. Bake 20 minutes or until the flesh is firm and flakes with a fork. (Hint: If onions begin to brown, catfish is done. Onions and peppers are strong flavored and will overpower fish if overused.)

Substitute Mrs. Dash Salt-free Table Blend seasoning for all of the spices and cover with onions and peppers.

Substitute lemon-pepper seasoning for all spices, and omit onions and peppers.

Cat Casserole

Keith Sutton

4 6- to 8-ounce catfish fillets
Salt, cayenne pepper
1 cup melted butter
1½ cups chopped green onions
½ cup diced celery
2 cups sliced fresh mushrooms
¾ cup dry cooking sherry
1 cup heavy whipping cream
¼ cup diced red pimientos
¾ cup grated Parmesan cheese
½ cup chopped pecans

Preheat oven to 400 degrees. Season fish with salt and cayenne; set aside. Add butter to a skillet and sauté green onions, celery, and mushrooms until wilted—about 3 to 5 minutes. Add sherry and stir well. Place catfish fillets on top of vegetables and cook 5 minutes without turning. Remove fillets to a baking dish and keep warm. Add cream to skillet and stir. Cook 5 minutes or till mixture has thickened. Pour sauce over catfish fillets, sprinkle with Parmesan cheese, pimientos, and pecans and place in oven until cheese is brown and fish flakes easily with a fork, approximately 10 minutes.

Catfish Gumbo

Keith Sutton

½ cup chopped celery
½ cup chopped onion
½ cup chopped green pepper
1 clove garlic, minced
¼ cup vegetable oil
4 cups beef broth
1 16-ounce can peeled tomatoes
1 10-ounce package frozen sliced okra
2 teaspoons salt
1 teaspoon black pepper
¼ teaspoon thyme
1 bay leaf
Louisiana hot sauce
1 pound catfish fillets
1½ cups hot cooked rice

Cook celery, onion, green pepper, and garlic in oil until tender. Add broth, tomatoes, okra, and seasonings. Cover and simmer 30 minutes. Cut catfish into 1-inch pieces and add. Cover and simmer 15 minutes longer or until fish flakes easily. Remove bay leaf. Place 1/4 cup rice in each of six soup bowls. Fill with gumbo.

Clembone's Catfish

Alan Clemons

Catfish fillets (3–4 pieces for each dinner guest)
4 cups Martha White Yellow Cornmeal
1 cup Martha White All-Purpose Flour
1 box Zatarains Spicy Fish Fry
4 large eggs
1 cup milk

Salt, pepper

⅛ teaspoon white pepper

2 gallons peanut oil

Wash fillets with cold water and remove bones, strips of fat, and red meat. Cut large fillets to thickness of ½ inch for even cooking. Pat dry and chill in refrigerator while preparing other items. Combine dry ingredients in paper bag. Combine eggs and milk in large bowl. Dip fillet in egg/milk wash, allow excess to drip off and drop fillet in paper bag. Do this with 5 to 6 fillets, then stir around with hand to thoroughly coat each fillet. Shake off excess and put fillet on a platter. After all fillets are coated, refrigerate for 20 to 30 minutes. Heat peanut oil in large pot on medium-high until a pinch of batter dropped in will bubble. Immerse 5 to 6 fillets at a time, cooking 3 to 5 minutes, and remove when golden brown. Serve with potato salad and coleslaw and enjoy.

Deep-Fried Flathead Catfish

Rob Weller

1 pound flathead catfish, cut into 4- to 5-inch strips

1 cup cornmeal

1 teaspoon salt

½ teaspoon pepper

¼ cup Parmesan cheese

hot sauce

oil

Wash and drain strips of flathead catfish. Place the flathead strips and dry ingredients in a paper sack and shake until the fish fillets are covered with the cornmeal mixture. Deep-fry fillets in oil for 5 to 10 minutes until golden brown. For added zing, top the cooked fillets with your favorite hot sauce.

Easy-Grilled Catfish

Keith Sutton

Any number of catfish fillets
Lemon-pepper spice

Season fillets with lemon-pepper. Place catfish in a well-oiled grill basket or on a well-oiled grill rack. Grill uncovered directly over medium-hot coals about 5 minutes per side or until fish flakes easily.

Fancy Cats

Tom Evans

3 to 6 pounds catfish fillets
½ cup mayonnaise
¼ teaspoon dried dill weed
1 teaspoon dehydrated onion
sea salt, pepper

Preheat oven to 350 degrees. Form pouch from aluminum foil, large enough to hold all fillets. Coat one side of fillets with mayonnaise and sprinkle with dill, sea salt, onion and pepper. Turn over and repeat. Put fillets in pouch, seal ends and bake 15 minutes. Open pouch with knife and broil 5 to 8 minutes, until fish flakes easily. Serve with salad, corn muffins, and iced tea. My, my, my!

Fried Catfish, Arkansas Style

Keith Sutton

¾ cup yellow cornmeal
¼ cup flour
2 teaspoons salt
½ teaspoon cayenne pepper
½ teaspoon garlic powder
2 pounds catfish fillets, steaks, or whole fish
peanut oil

Combine dry ingredients by shaking them together in a large plastic bag. Add catfish and shake to coat. Fill a cooker or skillet half full of peanut oil and heat to 365 degrees. Add catfish in a single layer, and fry until fish flakes easily with a fork—about 5 to 6 minutes. Remove and drain on paper towels.

Grilled Catfish

Tom Evans

3 to 6 pounds catfish fillets
2 cups zesty Italian bread crumbs
2 tablespoons Creole mustard
2 tablespoons olive oil
½ stick butter
salt, pepper

Cover grill with doubled aluminum foil. Brush foil with olive oil. Salt and pepper fillets and place on oil. Lightly cover fillets with Creole mustard. Mix bread crumbs in blender until fine. Melt butter and add to blender, and then mix again. Spread breadcrumb mix on fillets with knife and grill 20 minutes, with top closed, using medium, indirect heat. Will flake easily when done. Put on loose-fittin' britches and enjoy!

Grilled Flathead Catfish

Rob Weller

2 pounds flathead catfish fillets, no more than 1-inch thick
½ cup soy sauce
¼ cup brown sugar
1 tablespoon Worcestershire sauce
1 tablespoon fresh grated ginger
½ teaspoon garlic powder

Wash and drain flathead catfish fillets. Combine all other ingredients and marinate fillets 30 minutes to 1 hour before grilling. Wipe grill with vegetable oil to prevent sticking. Place fillets on heated grill and cook approximately 10 minutes on each side.

Quick Baked Catfish

Keith Sutton

2 pounds catfish fillets
½ cup mayonnaise
Bread crumbs
Paprika
Salt, pepper

Lightly coat fillets with mayonnaise; roll in bread crumbs. Place in a baking dish coated with nonstick cooking spray, and season to taste with paprika, salt, and pepper. Bake at 450 degrees for about 12 minutes or until fish flakes easily with fork.

Santee Swamp Catfish Stew

Walt Rhodes

2 to 3 pounds catfish fillets
1 to 2 pounds of Hillshire sausage, sliced
1 8-ounce can tomato paste
2 cans sliced okra
1 onion, diced
1 green pepper, diced
bacon, cooked and crumbled
2 or 3 cans diced tomatoes
1 large can whole tomatoes
2 to 3 cloves minced garlic
1 to 2 bay leaves
crushed red pepper, rosemary, thyme, oregano, tarragon

In a large pot, boil enough water to cover fish and then add fillets. Cook until done, at least 10 minutes. Skim off fat on top of water, and then drain. Put fillets back in pot and break into smaller pieces. Add remaining ingredients, spicing to taste, and mix. (No two pots are ever the same.) Bring mixture to a slow, low boil, reduce heat to low and simmer for 30 to 45 minutes, stirring frequently. Serve over white rice in bowls with hot sauce and cornbread. Stew is better the second day after it's cooled and reheated!

More Southern Hotspots

Alabama

Alabama River
Lake Eufaula
Lake Weiss
Tombigbee River

Arkansas

Millwood Lake
Lake Ouachita
St. Francis River
White River

Florida

Apalachicola River
Choctawhatchee
Escambia River
St. Johns River

Georgia

Coosa River
Lake Oconee
Lake Seminole
Savannah River

Kentucky

Barren River Lake
Green River
Kentucky River
Lake Herrington

Louisiana

Atchafalaya River
Cross Lake
Lac Des Allemands
Red River

Mississippi

Big Black River
Lake Tom Bailey
Pearl River
Tenn-Tom Waterway

Missouri

Grand River
Lake of the Ozarks
MDC Managed Impoundments
Table Rock Lake

North Carolina

Lake Norman
Lumber River
Neuse River
Yadkin River Lakes

South Carolina

Edisto River
Great Pee Dee River
SCDNR Fishing Lakes
Wateree River

Tennessee

Cherokee Lake
Family Fishing Lakes
Melton Hill Lake
Reelfoot Lake

Texas

Lake Lewisville
Lake O. H. Ivie
Lake Ray Hubbard
Possum Kingdom Lake

Virginia

Claytor Lake
Kerr Lake
New River
Occoquan Reservoir

West Virginia

Bluestone Lake
Kanawha River
New River
South Branch of the Potomac River

Catfishing in the South was designed and typeset on a Macintosh computer system using QuarkXPress software. The body text is set in 11/15 Goudy, and display type is set in Avant Garde. This book was designed and typeset by Cheryl Carrington and manufactured by Thomson-Shore, Inc.